CHURCH TRANSFUSION

CHURCH TRANSFUSION

Changing Your Church Organically—from the Inside Out

Neil Cole and Phil Helfer

Foreword by Dave Ferguson

JOSSEY-BASS
A Wiley Imprint
www.josseybass.com

Published by Jossey-Bass
A Wiley Imprint
One Montgomery Street, Suite 1200, San Francisco, CA 94104-4594—www.josseybass.com

Scripture quotations taken from the New American Standard Bible®, Copyright © 1960, 1962,
1963, 1968, 1971, 1972, 1973, 1975, 1977, 1995 by The Lockman Foundation. Used by permission.
(www.Lockman.org)

Jossey-Bass books and products are available through most bookstores. To contact Jossey-Bass
directly call our Customer Care Department within the U.S. at 800-956-7739, outside the U.S. at
317-572-3986, or fax 317-572-4002.

Wiley publishes in a variety of print and electronic formats and by print-on-demand. Some
material included with standard print versions of this book may not be included in e-books or in
print-on-demand. If this book refers to media such as a CD or DVD that is not included in the
version you purchased, you may download this material at http://booksupport.wiley.com. For more
information about Wiley products, visit www.wiley.com.

Library of Congress Cataloging-in-Publication Data
Cole, Neil, date
   Church transfusion : changing your church organically—from the inside out / Neil Cole and
Phil Helfer ; foreword by Dave Ferguson.
       p. cm. – (The Jossey-Bass leadership network series)
   Includes index.
     ISBN 978-1-118-13128-2 (hardback); ISBN 978-1-118-22509-7 (ebk; ISBN 978-1-118-23851-6 (ebk);
ISBN 978-1-118-26318-1 (ebk)
   1. Church renewal.   2. Church.   I. Helfer, Phil, 1958–   II. Title.
BV600.3.C635 2012
253–dc23
                                                                               2012017443

Printed in the United States of America
FIRST EDITION
HB Printing   10 9 8 7 6 5 4 3 2 1

Leadership Network Titles

The Blogging Church: Sharing the Story of Your Church Through Blogs, Brian Bailey
and Terry Storch

Church Turned Inside Out: A Guide for Designers, Refiners, and Re-Aligners,
Linda Bergquist and Allan Karr

*Leading from the Second Chair: Serving Your Church, Fulfilling Your Role, and
Realizing Your Dreams*, Mike Bonem and Roger Patterson

*In Pursuit of Great AND Godly Leadership: Tapping the Wisdom of the World for the
Kingdom of God,* Mike Bonem

Hybrid Church: The Fusion of Intimacy and Impact, Dave Browning

The Way of Jesus: A Journey of Freedom for Pilgrims and Wanderers,
Jonathan S. Campbell with Jennifer Campbell

*Cracking Your Church's Culture Code: Seven Keys to Unleashing Vision and
Inspiration,* Samuel R. Chand

*Leading the Team-Based Church: How Pastors and Church Staffs Can Grow Together
into a Powerful Fellowship of Leaders,* George Cladis

Organic Church: Growing Faith Where Life Happens, Neil Cole

Church 3.0: Upgrades for the Future of the Church, Neil Cole

Journeys to Significance: Charting a Leadership Course from the Life of Paul,
Neil Cole

Church Transfusion: Changing Your Church Organically—from the Inside Out,
Neil Cole and Phil Helfer

Off-Road Disciplines: Spiritual Adventures of Missional Leaders, Earl Creps

*Reverse Mentoring: How Young Leaders Can Transform the Church and Why We
Should Let Them,* Earl Creps

*Building a Healthy Multi-Ethnic Church: Mandate, Commitments, and Practices of a
Diverse Congregation,* Mark DeYmaz

Leading Congregational Change Workbook, James H. Furr, Mike Bonem, and
Jim Herrington

The Tangible Kingdom: Creating Incarnational Community, Hugh Halter and
Matt Smay

*Baby Boomers and Beyond: Tapping the Ministry Talents and Passions of Adults over
Fifty,* Amy Hanson

Leading Congregational Change: A Practical Guide for the Transformational Journey,
Jim Herrington, Mike Bonem, and James H. Furr

*The Leader's Journey: Accepting the Call to Personal and Congregational
Transformation,* Jim Herrington, Robert Creech, and Trisha Taylor

The Permanent Revolution: Apostolic Imagination and Practice for the 21st Century,
Alan Hirsch and Tim Catchim

1410

126494

CONTENTS

About the Jossey-Bass Leadership Network Series

Leadership Network's mission is to accelerate the impact of 100X leaders. These high-capacity leaders are like the hundredfold crop that comes from seed planted in good soil as Jesus described in Matthew 13:8.

Leadership Network

- Explores the "what's next?" of what could be
- Creates "aha!" environments for collaborative discovery
- Works with exceptional "positive deviants"
- Invests in the success of others through generous relationships
- Pursues big impact through measurable kingdom results
- Strives to model Jesus through all we do

Believing that meaningful conversations and strategic connections can change the world, we seek to help leaders navigate the future by exploring new ideas and finding application for each unique context. Through collaborative meetings and processes, leaders map future possibilities and challenge one another to action that accelerates fruitfulness and effectiveness. Leadership Network shares the learnings and inspiration with others through our books, concept papers, research reports, e-newsletters, podcasts, videos, and online experiences. This in turn generates a ripple effect of new conversations and further influence.

In 1996, Leadership Network established a partnership with Jossey-Bass, a Wiley Imprint, to develop a series of creative books that would provide thought leadership to innovators in church ministry. *Leadership Network Publications* present *thoroughly researched and innovative concepts* from leading thinkers, practitioners, and pioneering churches.

To learn more about Leadership Network go to www .leadnet.org.

FOREWORD

Dave Ferguson

I was sure there would be a fight! I was afraid the Exponential Conference, the largest church planting conference in the country, might end up looking more like an Ultimate Fighting Championship. In one corner, for the first time ever, we had pulled together leaders from the missional-incarnational crowd who advocated for churches being simple, small, and reproducible. And in the other corner we had church-planting leaders trained in the church growth model that believed in launching churches as large as possible. We had both sides represented in several panels; we had thought-leaders cofacilitating workshops and everyone expected sparks to fly, controversy to ensue, and hand grenades to be lobbed back and forth. None of that happened. I'm not sure a single punch was landed. In fact, after I finished leading my workshop with Neil Cole at that Exponential Conference I remember him looking me in the eye and saying, *"Dave, for a mega, multisite church guy, you are not too bad!"* That workshop was the beginning of my friendship with Neil Cole. But long before that he was a significant influence in my life and in my leadership through his writing and his practice as an apostolic leader and Christ follower. I continue to read everything Neil writes and pay very close attention to all he says. I believe Neil is not only an apostolic leader but also a prophetic voice that gives us a glimpse of God's church as it's meant to be.

So what happened to all the controversy at Exponential? There was no controversy; but there was the beginning of a very important Kingdom conversation about how all churches can become missional movements just as Jesus intended. Because of Neil and other missional leaders like him, I have been on a journey with the church I lead, Community Christian Church, and the church-planting network for which I provide vision,

NewThing. During the last two years I've been sharing what I've learned in this conversation through a process called "Future Travelers." This is a process that is helping churches make the shift toward becoming a missional movement. During the last twenty-four months I've discovered there are at least three critical moves these churches must make to make that shift:

Move toward practices that apprentice people in the ways of Jesus.

Move toward clearly understanding and articulating the mission of Jesus.

Move toward a vision of a movement to accomplish the Jesus mission.

Some churches "get" one of the three. Very few "get" two. None of them "get" all three, and most "get" none. If you are a church leader who wants to see your people apprenticed in the ways of Jesus; if you desire to see your energy and effort contribute to the mission of Jesus; if you long to be a part of a missional movement, then *Church Transfusion: Changing Your Church Organically—from the Inside Out* will show you how.

And that is why *Church Transfusion* is so important. Within the pages of this book is both the encouragement to make the shift and the practical application for how to make this shift from authors who do "get it."

Now, I don't agree with everything Neil says or writes. Check out the shots he takes at multisite in Chapter Eleven. And he doesn't endorse everything I say or write. But I need Neil Cole. I need his influence and I need to be in conversation with him because he understands the church as a missional movement!

So, throw down your boxing gloves, stop being defensive and enter into an important Kingdom conversation. I believe *Church Transfusion: Changing Your Church Organically* is the latest discussion in this important conversation about the church as a missional movement. If we take this book and missional movement seriously we will see in the twenty-first-century church in the west what we saw in the first-century church in the east.

Dave Ferguson
Lead Pastor, Community Christian Church
and Visionary of NewThing

PREFACE

Neil Cole

Many people have considered me to be against the established church. They see me as a purist who only believes that organic churches meeting in homes or places of business are the true church. Those who thought this way will be surprised by this book.

My coauthor, Phil Helfer, has been my partner in founding and leading our movement from the beginning. We have worked together for over twenty years now. Phil is one of the most radical organic theologians I have met (and I have met many). But he also pastors a congregation of 250 to 300 people that meets on Sundays in a fifty-year-old building with pews, a pulpit, a choir, and Sunday school. That sounds about as traditional as can be, doesn't it? Yet Phil and I have been working together to develop the concepts of organic church from the start. If the way people often think of me is true and I am simply a house church purist, then there is no way that Phil and I could start and lead this ministry together. Whatever we have developed in the organic church greenhouse training, which teaches people how to start organic churches by making disciples where there were none before, is applied in Phil's context as much as my own. You will see that clearly in this book.

We both love the church, and we always have. I have written that those who bash the bride had best be careful because sooner or later they will have to take on the groom. This is certainly not a book about how to change a traditional expression of church into house churches. I do not see the church as only valid in the house church model. In fact, we do not think that organic church is a model at all but rather a mind-set. We believe that every church is organic—or it's not the church.

That said, I am a purist when it comes to talking about what actually is the organic nature of the church and what releases that healthy DNA of Christ's body to become the movement it was meant to be. If you were thinking that this book might let you off the hook for the ways you are currently doing church, you may be disappointed. We will not attack any model of church, but at the same time we will not condone unhealthy practices that are preventing the church from becoming healthy and reproducing naturally. The very idea of change requires that one admit that the current forms or practices are not working well.

In a way, while I am not strictly a house church purist, I am a purist on what is needed if the church is to become healthy and begin to reproduce and ignite movements. I am not picky about church models, but I am picky on what the cure for our lack of health is. Jesus is the cure, not any model of church, but there are some models that can multiply spontaneously and others that cannot. I have always said that and always will. Our standard church practices will accomplish only what they have been accomplishing, and that is not good enough by any stretch of the imagination. So this book is about change. We do not suggest that you change to house churches but that churches should become simpler, more organic, disciple-making spiritual families that reproduce.

We are writing this book for all those churches that already exist in whatever form. We want to help them know how to transfuse a healthy and organic DNA that can replicate health and life.

If you have read some of my other works, you will find some ideas repeated here, but placed in an entirely new context. So you will see some familiar concepts but cast with new light and application. The concepts I have committed my life to remain, to my own mind, universal and absolute. Because of the nature of this project, you will also find brand-new material that is not found in any of my other works. Even if you read all my other books, this one will contribute new material to your understanding and also reinforce ideas elaborated in other books. This is in no way a rehash of other material.

You will find in this book all the same passion in my earlier works, but the starting place is radically different. Bringing organic transfusion to an established church is a wholly different process from starting something from scratch. While my values, theology, and practices remain consistent in this book, the place where we start is radically different and therefore requires a different pathway to reach our goal.

Most books on the subject of revitalizing churches have a different goal than we do in this book. In most cases the resources are written for plateaued or declining churches to help them grow larger in attendance. This book will not lay out the variety of kinds of churches and stress different practical steps to become more attractive to more people. This book will not describe ways to motivate unmotivated people to do what they don't want to do. You'll find nothing of that sort in this volume.

For us, church growth is not a solution, nor is it success. We want to see healthy disciples reproducing other healthy disciples, leaders emerging, and new churches being born that will reproduce spontaneously. If that is not your goal, and you simply want to have a growth spurt in attendance, there are plenty of other books you should read.

In fact, this book may be a good book to read even if your church is growing rapidly and considered a success but you are not content with that because you want to be part of a movement. We believe that what we will share is important for any church and any model to become more authentically organic and release vital disciples into the world to affect neighborhoods and nations.

If you are part of an established church, growing or not, and look at the rapidly spreading movement of organic churches with a degree of longing but also with a deep-seated obligation to the congregation you are currently called to, this book can be good news for you. If you read the book of Acts and then go to church Sunday and realize that these two stories are as different as the sun is from the moon, then this book may be helpful. If you remember when you first felt called to serve Christ and the enthusiasm you had then to see the world changed and now you just fulfill a job description, you have chosen the right book to read. If your church is badly in need of a fresh infusion of life that spills out into the streets, this book is in the right hands.

Neil Cole

June 2012   Long Beach, California

This book is dedicated to those pastors who are frustrated because they have found themselves stuck in an institution that is choking the life and fruitfulness out of their ministry and are now willing to take the radical steps necessary to release that life. Take courage, stand firm, and fight the good fight—you will reap if you do not grow weary.

ACKNOWLEDGMENTS

From Neil: I wish to thank my coauthor on this project, Phil. We are cofounders of Church Multiplication Associates, coworkers for more than twenty years, and now he is my coauthor as well. I wish to honor him not just for his role in this ministry and in writing this book but also for being an example of all that this book entails. Phil, you have been my friend, my cofounder, my coauthor, and always my pastor. Thanks.

I want to thank my spiritual family during the 1990s, Grace Fellowship of Alta Loma, who provided this rookie pastor with lots of opportunities for mistakes and lessons that can only be learned through experience. It has been several years now since I inflicted you all with these lessons, but the impact you have had on my life will never diminish, and many of those lessons are reflected in this writing. Thank you.

I also want to thank Brad and Cari Fieldhouse for the blessing of hospitality I received while writing this book. A strange quirk of mine is that once I write a book in a place, I am unable to write another book in that place. Why? I don't know, but it is frustrating, and can be expensive. When my oldest daughter moved out, my wife turned her old bedroom into a beautiful home office for me to write in, which I did, and *Church 3.0* is the result. Now I can't write another book there because every time I sit there to write, I am reminded so much of *Church 3.0* that I can't get my mind thinking on the next project. When I was not making much progress on this book, Brad and Cari offered a place for me to have a writing retreat, and the momentum finally kicked in. For that I am very grateful. Oh, and Brad and Cari, you don't have to worry about another future invasion; I can't write anything else in your guest room.

That reminds me, anyone else have a place I can retreat to? I still have more books in me, but I need some new places to write in.

From Phil: I wish to thank my coauthor and fellow laborer in the fields for all the years we've walked together on this spiritual journey. God has made us brothers in the most intimate sense of the word. Thanks, Neil, for putting up with me and giving me the chance to work with you on this project.

I am extremely grateful to my family: my wife, Lori, for being my sounding board, listening to my crazy ideas, asking the right questions, and urging me on to further discoveries, and our girls, Jenna, Haley and Stacey, for listening to me week after week and asking the questions that matter. I've learned more from raising you than you will ever know. You guys are the best!

I'd also like to thank my spiritual family, the people of God known as Los Altos Grace Brethren Church, for embracing and implementing the principles in this book. Without you all, our transfusion would never have taken hold, and this book would never have been written. I am especially grateful to the leaders who have been willing to open their minds and hearts and step into the flow of God's kingdom. Pete, Dave, Chuck, Mike M., Bill, Mike J., Ric, Allen, and Rick: we have fought the good fight side by side and will continue to do so. May the Lord grant us the privilege of seeing His rule flourish in the hearts of His people!

A special thanks too to Karen, Cindi, and Marianne. You are all tireless workers who are constantly busy doing the things He's called you to do, and yet you still find time to keep me in line and on task.

From both of us: Last, we would like to thank all the guys at CMA, especially Ed, Dezi, Chris, Paul, and Mike. We have spent many years learning to follow Christ together. You guys are an inspiration to us, and this book comes out of the lessons He's taught us along the way.

Church Transfusion

PART ONE

CHANGE IS POSSIBLE— WITH GOD

CHAPTER ONE

SO WHAT'S THE DIFFERENCE?

There are some common characteristics in every culture around the world. Every culture has a religious element within it—and alcohol. Whether we like it or not, God exists, and we are all accountable to Him. That alone can drive some to drink.

Every religion, whether Buddhism, Islam, Judaism, Hinduism, or any variety of cult or sect you can find, has some common elements as well. You will find some holy sites with a special building erected there for religious ceremony and ritual. You will find a few special people called, trained, and financially supported to do the perfunctory religious practices for the good of all the members of the religion—usually dressed in special robes and headgear to separate them from the common folk. You will find a religious hierarchical caste system in every religion of the world. You will find that people must observe certain practices to gain approval of their God or gods, all as preparation for their impending future judgment in the afterlife. There will be some holy days and some holy ceremonies conducted at the holy sanctuary that the holy men preside over.

You will also find all these same elements within Christianity. But the question is, should we? Is Christianity just another religion like all the others? Or is there to be a stark difference? We believe that the kingdom of God is always meant to stand out as vastly different from everything else, which are in fact counterfeits put forward to entice people away from the real truth. We believe that we have allowed the world to co-opt and corrupt the true and vital expression of life in Christ and substitute it with the same old religious system found everywhere else in the world. How tragic is that?

If you read the Bible, you will find that the New Testament does not establish religious holy days, a clergy system, a sacred building, or a meritorious set of practices that all must conform to in order to gain the requisite favor of God. In fact, what the New Testament does is quite the opposite: it fulfills all the previous requirements from the Old Testament and then releases something so new and different that it stands out from all the world has to offer as radically new and different and is impossible to stop in its pure form.

The old covenant pointed to the need and reality of a coming new covenant that would provide a true and complete salvation and transformation. The old covenant could not save. In the old religious system, people were motivated to behave better through guilt, shame, and fear. These things never saved anyone but only demonstrated our need of a savior.

All the other religious systems of the world try to conform people to a standard of behavior fitting for its own rules and worldview. Getting people to act correctly is the desired outcome. Removing bad or potentially negative choices is one way to accomplish this behavior modification. We end up with rules such as "Don't dance, don't drink, don't chew—and don't go out with girls that do." Many a "Christian" college has its students sign a covenant that they will not dance, drink, play cards, or go to the movies while they are enrolled. All of this is an attempt to control people's choices so that they do not make wrong ones.

The new covenant puts God's Word in our hearts so that we actually want to live the truth. The new covenant adopts us as children into God's family and gives us all the inheritance of his kingdom without any merit on our part. We are blessed with every spiritual blessing and given everything we need for life and godliness. The very Spirit of God is placed within us as a pledge of all that is ours in Christ. No longer do we do good works out of fear, guilt, or shame but because Christ has freely provided a full and complete salvation with nothing left to be earned from God, we are now free to love both God and others. We do not do good to merit blessings; we are fully blessed, and so we are now able to love without any selfish motivation. We have nothing to gain by our love because we have already gained everything possible without first deserving it. Why would we want to sign a covenant to conform in our behavior when we have already been given everything the new covenant has to offer, a powerful presence that can actually transform us from within?

Love is the only way to fulfill the Law. Obligation, duty, guilt, shame, fear, inspiration, pride, emotional appeals—none of these things are sufficient to meet the obligations of the Law.

Love is always a choice; it is never just a duty. When a couple get to the point where they are carrying on under obligation and duty, it is common for the wife to ask, "Don't you love me anymore?" When the husband says, "Of course I love you. I married you, didn't I?" he will not find that response gaining him any favor. Why? Because love is a choice, and a choice is something that you make every day, not just once in the past. Every wife wants to be a chosen bride every day. She wants her husband to choose her over his friends, over his career, over his favorite team, over his X-Box, over his smart phone—every day. That is love to her. Love is a choice. Try telling your spouse that you love her or him because you said you would and now you have to because you are under contract. See if that scores you any points. It won't—precisely because love is a choice and not a duty.

The thing about a choice is that by definition, you have options. In essence, you cannot choose to love without the possibility of choosing not to love.

Parents (or pastors) who work hard to remove all the possible negative options so that their children can only make good choices are using a form of behavior modification. This practice may result in good moral people but will fail to produce people who choose to love freely. Christianity is meant for so much more than sin management! When you remove the wicked options from people, you also remove love as a possibility. There is a reason that God left the tree of the knowledge of good and evil in the garden with Adam and Eve. He wanted them (and us) to love him, to choose him, and to do that he had to risk our choosing wrongly. Christianity without choice is a Christianity without love. A Christianity without love is a counterfeit, and a poor one at that. Jesus warns the church of the Ephesians that they were dangerously close to being removed from his presence because they had left their first love (Rev. 2:1–9). Nothing short of repentance is in order for a situation such as this.

Morality is simply not enough. Charles H. Spurgeon is said to have remarked, "Morality may keep you out of jail, but it takes the blood of Jesus Christ to keep you out of hell." The righteousness of Christ is of a wholly different nature. True righteousness flows from the inside out, and no amount of behavior modification can cause it—or stop it.

It is time to abandon the domestic faith of suburban consumer Churchianity to live a life of risk for the love of a Savior who left heaven to live among the poor and marginalized people of a backward and oppressed nation. The true Jesus is not a safe and sterile milquetoast wimp, conflicted by an inner tension between a mission and a passive kindness—which Hollywood typically portrays and Christians are comfortable believing in. He said things that offended others regularly. He never followed the party line. Jesus shocked his foes, his friends, and his followers in equal doses.

In their book *Untamed,* Alan and Debra Hirsch say, "His was a wild holiness that calls all to account who refuse to deal with God but prefer to follow the lame dictates of a religion of ethical codes and pious rituals."[1]

The Hirsches then go on to pose a revealing question and counterquestion that opens our eyes to the tamed existence we have grown accustomed to:

> What is it about the holiness of Jesus that caused "sinners" to flock to him like a magnet and yet manages to seriously antagonize the religious people? This question begs yet another, even more confronting question: why does our more churchy form of holiness seem to get it the other way around?

They go on to explain:

> One of the greatest counterfeits for following the untamed Jesus comes from the substitution of morals and decency for Jesus' untamed kind of holiness. One of the standard attempts to stereotype, and therefore domesticate, Jesus is to make him into a moral Teacher, someone who taught us how to live decent, rule-based lives.[2]

The holiness of God is much more than a tamed and moral existence. Jesus was on a mission not to rescue those who were moral but those who were broken and imprisoned by evil; in fact, they are one and the same, the only difference being that the moral people are unaware of their spiritual bankruptcy and bondage. He was destined to reach into dark and sin-infested places to call out and redeem the beautiful image of God found in people who were enslaved by evil. He did not hang out in safe places. I imagine that today you would be more likely to find Jesus in a gay bar than at a church service. When he would go to the religious service, he might be likely to overturn the book and T-shirt tables and chase away the salespeople. He risked his reputation to be with the people that needed saving and knew they did. This is our Savior. His mission has not been altered or changed in two thousand years, and he bids us to join Him. Are you willing to walk into some dangerous places with Jesus at your back? It is always a choice.

The power of the gospel has done away with the useless religious mechanisms that didn't work then and still don't work now and replaced them with a vital faith, motivated by love.

Love at its core is unselfish devotion to another. Love makes a person willing to put their own need aside and focus on doing what's best for another. Love seeks the highest good for the object of its affection. The opposite of love is selfishness. Selfishness looks out for number one and causes a person to focus merely on his or her own interests and needs. God desires for His children to love each other and also to love Him. He recognized that this would be impossible as long as there was something people needed to get from Him. This is why we believe God made salvation free. Think about it. Through one act of love, the death, burial, and resurrection of Christ, God has provided mankind with forgiveness, eternal life, everything necessary for life and godliness, and every spiritual blessing in the heavenly places in Christ Jesus. There is nothing left for the one who has faith in Christ to receive. Those He called He also justified, sanctified, and glorified. Our eternal inheritance is reserved in heaven and protected by the power of God. Everything has been provided through the loving service of Jesus Christ. There is nothing left to earn.

If anything had been left to earn—God's love or acceptance, for example—our efforts to do His will would be, of necessity, selfish. As we worked to accomplish His goals, our motives would be suspect. We would always be seeking to get what was lacking for ourselves. But God, in His wisdom, removed this obstacle. He gave those who believe in Him absolutely everything as a gift up front. There is nothing left for us to get from God. We have already received every possible spiritual blessing. The finished work of Christ is all that's necessary.

Because everything we will ever get is already ours, we can serve God without selfishness. We are free to seek for His highest good and the good of His kingdom without the need to seek anything for ourselves. This is love, and it's meant to be the distinguishing mark of every Christ follower, every church, and the entire Christian movement (John 13:34–35). But love is always a choice and never a guilt-ridden obligation, so we can choose not to love, as destructive as that is.

It's what makes us different from the rest of the world, but unfortunately, it hasn't seemed to accomplish the job. Why? Because like dogs returning to their vomit, we have gone back to the old covenant and chosen a religion like all the others instead of the true thing. Like Israel, we want to go back to Egypt instead of following a pillar of fire by night, a pillar of smoke by day, and eating supernatural food as we watch God do the miraculous at every turn. Instead we choose the same old religious systems that every other rank-and-file world religion offers, the only difference being that we use a cross as our symbol.

Why would you want to give up the daily miracle of God's actual presence and leading, a presence that parts oceans and causes water to flow from rocks or breaks the political oppression of Pharaoh? Why would we want to be like everyone else on the planet when we could live a supernatural life of love every day? Why would we choose a human hierarchical system, monitoring and controlling our actions over the actual living presence of Christ leading, guiding, and providing every day? Why would we substitute a dark and cold cathedral floor for the glory of constantly walking on the holy ground of Christ's presence?

This book, at its core, is about a choice—a choice made every day. God has loved us with an everlasting, abundantly sufficient love. Will we sell our birthright like Esau and be content with something that looks, smells, and sounds like every other religion of the world, or will we claim what has been given to us and allow something fresh, powerful, and dynamic to flow through us, reaching far beyond the boundaries of our control or oversight?

One thing is clear: you cannot continue in the old covenant and hope to experience new covenant results. If you truly want the life Jesus died to give to both you and your church, you have to trust his wisdom and love and stop living by the old ways that merely pump out the same old domesticated Christians who have failed to make much of a difference in this world. The Law is no substitute for grace. The power of sin is the Law, and the free gift of God is eternal life.

Jesus has always intended for His movement to be more than it appears to be. The kingdom of God is meant to be an unstoppable apostolic movement carried forward by each and every follower of Christ. Our current religious systems are not that. There are people in your church who long to be part of the real thing. Perhaps you want to be part of it as well. We must start to let go of what is to launch into what can be, and this may be the start. If what we have been doing for the past hundred years hasn't produced a movement yet, why on earth would we keep on doing what we have been doing? Our current systems are perfectly designed to produce the results we are currently getting. It is time for a change, time for church as we know it to be transfused with the power and presence of the living God.

The Upside-Down Kingdom

Lest you think that Christianity is different from all the other religions as it stands now because it has a better doctrine, let us simply point out some of the radically upside-down things Jesus said about His kingdom so you can see how far removed we really are. What is characteristic about each of these statements is how opposite they are from natural thinking—and from the thinking in the church of the West.

The way to get big is to go small. All multiplication movements begin small. Jesus described His kingdom as starting with the smallest seed known to man at the time–the mustard seed. All reproduction occurs on the cellular level. In essence, if the cells of your body are not healthy, your body is unhealthy. It doesn't matter if you have a killer wardrobe, a facelift, and a winning smile on the outside if the cells that make up your body are ailing. While most pastors are considering ways to get a bigger church, the key to true success is to go smaller. In the end, if you get the small things right, global impact will eventually come. When it comes to church transfusion, you must begin by planting health in the smallest unit of church life–the disciple in relation to other disciples. If you can't multiply at that level, you will never multiply at any larger and more complicated level.

The way to go fast is to start slow. Exponential growth always starts slow. A large and fast start may be appealing for most church planters, but that actually negates the possibility that the work they are doing might ever become a spontaneously multiplying movement. All multiplication starts off slow and builds in momentum with each succeeding generation: 2 becomes 4; 4 becomes 8; 8 becomes 16; . . . There's nothing impressive about these numbers at first, but by the fifteenth year, you have 32,768. By the twentieth year, you have passed a million and just keep on going. By the time you pass the thirty-fourth year, you have reached every person on the planet and have started reaching out to new solar systems. This is basic math. In church transfusion you must respect the long, slow beginning that is a part of the multiplication process. If you bypass the slow beginning, you bypass multiplication. Most church leaders grow impatient with the slow start of multiplication and feel that they are failing, so they instead opt for a fast addition approach. Once that decision is made, the future of the church is likely stuck in addition mode and will probably never produce real multiplication.

The way to be strong is to become weak. Success can often become your greatest hindrance in a church. Does that sound strange? The spiritual truth is clear in the Scriptures: the stronger we are, the weaker we become spiritually. True spiritual strength comes in weakness. Success is sometimes a tool of the devil that spawns pride, self-sufficiency, and an inability to learn anything new. A person or church that acknowledges its weakness is more likely to turn to God for help. One who is self-sufficient is further from dependence on God for the fulfillment of needs. In church transfusion it is harder to get a church that thinks it is strong to accept that it needs a transfusion. Jesus said, "It is not the well who need a physician but those who are sick."

The way to becoming rich is to give everything away. The more you cling to, the less you will have. Greed is not the way to have plenty in God's kingdom. The more generous one is, the more riches one will truly have. One who has nothing to lose is a dangerous person. Jesus said, "Where your treasure is, there will your heart be also." When a church starts to accumulate things and hold on to them as prizes worth defending or preserving, they will quickly find that their affection and provision is not found in Christ but in the maintenance and management of possessions and property. In church transfusion we have found over and over again that the church that holds loosely to all its assets and gives generously is the church that is healthy and is one that God would prefer to multiply.

The way to be first is to be last. It is the American way to push and pull yourself to the top of the ladder. We have annual articles in our Christian magazines ranking our successes as the fastest-growing churches or the largest churches. We even occasionally have lists of the fifty most influential people. Jesus was never impressed with these things. He clearly says that the way to be first is to become the last. Most of the church growth occurring in America is merely transfer growth at the expense of other churches. The current mood of Christendom is that of competition, where each church is striving to grow with little to no regard for the church that is losing its members to the growing church. In church transfusion, the leadership needs not to pursue being above others but to lift others up. In fact, if a church were more concerned with the success of the church around the corner than its own success, we firmly believe that God would honor such a church with fruitfulness. Test us on this; we dare you.

The way to live is to die. In God's kingdom resurrection is meant to be the way to life. In church transfusion we must die to our old ways if we hope to exist in new resurrected ways. This truth is universal and applies to us as individuals and to us as a collective—the church. All change begins with a death. A church that is unwilling to risk death is simply unwilling to live by faith in Christ. Resurrection power is available only to the person or church that is willing to die. Death is no longer our enemy, for there is no sting in death anymore. When we place our faith in our own efforts to maintain the life of the church, we have already passed into a place of dying. We of all people should be ready to embrace death as if our life depended on it—because it does. Jesus said, "Whoever clings to his life will lose it, and whoever loses his life for my sake gains it." All church transfusion begins with the concept of death. The churches that are more ready to die are the healthier churches. In most churches and ministries of the West, leadership is focused on self-preservation and keeping things going. Decisions are based on how the outcome will help the church continue. Those who are in self-preservation mode are dead already; they just don't know it yet. As our friend Lance Ford once said, "You need more than buy-in to change a church; you need die-in."

ABOUT CHURCH TRANSFUSION

The life is in the blood, and the life for Christ's body is in His blood. We need more than an organizational transition; we need a full transfusion of Jesus' blood, His life, within every disciple. Anything less than that will only perpetuate more of the dysfunction and unhealthy church practices that have already plagued us for far too long. We are in desperate need of the internally transforming power of the gospel of grace and the presence of Christ so that our salvation is then worked out in a way the rest of the world will see. It isn't enough that we believe in the facts contained in the gospel; we must allow the gospel itself to infect our souls and transform us from within. The DNA of Jesus' lifeblood is needed in our churches, and nothing shy of a full transfusion that touches every cell will be sufficient.

In this book we will first point out that change is possible with God, but only with God. Frankly, if change is possible by human efforts, it is not even worth pursuing. In the second half of the book we will lay out some of the actual practical considerations to weigh if you want to release real organic health in your church.

Jesus didn't die and rise from the dead so that we can be like everyone else in the world. Our faith is more than just a better doctrine; it is a better life. Jesus is the difference, and what a difference he makes! Don't be satisfied with less.

CHAPTER TWO

BASIC ORGANIC PRINCIPLES THAT WORK IN ALL CONTEXTS

"It's far easier to give birth than it is to raise the dead." Many years ago, while considering what course I (Neil) should pursue in church ministry, I heard that statement, and it has stuck with me to this day. A missionary said those words to me, and I think that it had a lot to do with why I chose church planting as a long-range course for my life. I have been highly invested in the planting of churches for the past twenty-one years. My experience, training, books, articles, and lectures have all been focused on starting healthy churches that will reproduce healthy disciples and other healthy churches.

Giving birth, mind you, is no easy task—just ask your own mother—but it is far more common and probable than raising the dead. In recent days, however, I have come to realize that while I love Christmas, I think that Easter is also a special celebration. One has to do with birth, the other with resurrection. God delights in both, and so should we. This book is directed at the resurrection side of church work.

Not that I am entirely one-sided on the issue of church planting. I spent more than eight years as a pastor of an established church that made great strides toward being reborn into a healthy incarnation. I learned a lot during those years, and I only hope that the beloved people there learned at least a few things from me as well. So as I write into the resurrection side of the church world, I do so with some experience and insight forged in the pain and joy that is felt with death, burial, and resurrection.

Before we go any further, there are a few principles we have to establish. Some of the content in this chapter may be review for readers who are familiar with our books but is worth repeating and specifically contextualizing for an established church environment.

When we speak of the church, we are not speaking of groups organized for worship, evangelism, or anything else but rather we are talking of that wonderful creation of God that was born at Pentecost and is yet to mature fully. It has its visible expression in the many and various families of Christ followers throughout the centuries and around the globe. The church is a living, growing entity made up of all who belong to Jesus and are led by His Spirit.

For too many people, the church has become synonymous with other groups that are organized around a specific purpose. For example, there are groups that feed the poor, house the homeless, help the jobless find jobs, and on and on. The church is often seen in the world (even by those who lead it) as a group organized around this sort of purpose. Church leaders dress it up with pretty-sounding words like *worship, outreach, evangelism, Christian education,* and *community service.* Although a church may be called to do all of these things, it was never meant to be organized around them. What the church does and what the church is are two very different things.

When we organize a church around what it does, the focus is shifted from Christ as the source of direction and power to the church itself as an avenue of service to God. We begin to see our own creative efforts as the primary means to accomplish some great thing that can then be delivered to God as some sort of offering. We become the source of the effort, and He becomes the recipient of the work of our hands.

The Scriptures present the church as a body with Christ as its head. Not only does this metaphor imply that the church is alive but also that it derives its life from the Lord Himself. If Jesus is the Head, then every part must be connected to Him and obeying His direction for the body to be healthy and growing. If you take a head off a human body, the body will die. If you somehow disrupt the communication between the head and the body, the part of the body that is isolated will either become dormant or will act out on its own. Either way, that part of the body will no longer be able to fulfill its purpose and will likely become a liability to the rest of the body as well.

If there is a communication breakdown between the head and the body, the body suffers and becomes useless. The church works the same way. Every believer must be connected to the Head. All must be taught that Jesus is their leader and the source of their life, and they must be released to follow Him.

When a church understands its place of submission to Christ as its Head and leader, attention is shifted away from accomplishing *our* goals and is focused on Him and His direction, guidance, and power. What the church does becomes about what God wants and how He wants it done.

Both of us are from the same denomination, the Fellowship of Grace Brethren Churches. When our denomination held a retreat for local pastors a few years back, we spent three days together trying to answer the question "What is church?" At the end of our time we were amazed that we could not find agreement on the very nature of this thing we each felt called to lead.

Some of our disagreements centered around whether or not official leadership was necessary or whether or not certain ordinances had to be practiced. Other issues had to do with such things as incorporation, size, number and types of leaders present, property, buildings, budgets, the presence of certain spiritual gifts (including administration, of course), and I'm sure you can imagine the rest.

This discussion opened our eyes to just how much trouble we are really in. If we don't understand what the church is, how can we ever lead it effectively?

With much study, research, experience, and time spent seeking wisdom from smarter men than us, we have come to understand church by this simple yet profound description: "The church is the presence of Jesus among His people, called out as a spiritual family, to pursue His mission on this planet."[1]

The Bible uses a number of metaphors to describe the nature of the church. The church is described, among other things, as salt and light, a bride, a family, a flock, a field of wheat, a mustard seed, branches connected to a vine, leaven, a body, and a building.

These metaphors have one very striking thing in common. They all imply that the church is a living thing. What about the building, you might ask. Remember, it's built with living stones and is a dwelling place for the Living God.

The church is alive, and Jesus in its midst is its life. What is a body without a head? A corpse. What is a bride without a groom? A widow. What is a branch without a vine? Firewood. What is a building without a foundation? Rubble. What is a flock without a shepherd? A wolf's all-you-can-eat buffet. Every New Testament picture of the church points to a living connection with Jesus as the most essential component of its being.

God's presence is not just a necessary part of the definition of church; it is the most essential one. It is the starting place and the one thing that separates the church from any other organization or institution on the planet. This important connection can be seen from the beginning of the church in Acts to its threatened end found in the book of Revelation. In Acts 1 the believers were together; they had been instructed to pray, worship, and practice the ordinances; and they had appointed leadership, but they were instructed not to leave the upper room. Church was born in Acts 2. What's the only ingredient added in Acts 2 to establish the church? It is the presence of the Spirit of Jesus in each follower that was the breath of life that animated the body of Christ. The threatened demise of the Ephesian church in Revelation 2:1–7 is that it be removed from the presence of Jesus, which would be the end of that church.

If the church is a living thing, then it has to be treated differently from your run-of-the-mill organization. Living things are organized differently from nonliving things.

For decades the church in America and many other parts of the world has been treated like a business. Principles of business management have been used to help the church grow and accomplish its mission. Pastors have been transformed into CEOs and church members into spiritual consumers. We sincerely believe that many churches are more concerned about market share than they are about bringing light and life to a dark and dying world. Think about the focus of the average church. For most, it's all about Sunday services. Regardless of which day or days you meet or how many times you meet per week, the same issue remains. The time and energies of church leaders are consumed by the need to produce some sort of event that will appeal to a certain constituency. In other words, they spend their time creating spiritual goods and services to be provided to and consumed by a spiritual marketplace.

Churches find they are in competition with other churches, but we ask, is this actually possible in the body of Christ? It is as if Christ's body is suffering from some autoimmune disorder that has us attacking ourselves for our own self-interest, and in the end the whole body suffers. If the church is Christ's body and bride, can it be established at the expense of itself? Any church that is in competition for a market share of a finite constituency in a given target population is propagating a business rather than a body.

Large churches with large resources are able to do this very well. This enables them to increase their market share of the spiritual goods and services offered to a consuming public while the smaller churches struggle to keep people from leaving for the bigger churches' more polished products.

As a by-product of this unseemly enterprise, many pastors of smaller churches have become disheartened and defeated. Week after week they pour what resources they have into creating products they hope will satisfy the ever more picky churchgoer, only to find that they can't keep up. What to do?

Many pastors address these issues by attending seminars and reading books that claim to hold the secret to escaping this vicious cycle by growing their church. The elusive promise is that if we can just get big enough so as to have enough resources to throw at creating better, more attractive products and services, our church (company) will finally be able to compete. Even when it works (which is rare), it does nothing to solve the basic problem. Churches were never meant to become providers of spiritual goods and services to consumers, even if there are many who appear more than eager to buy.

In our present situation, we have a provider class (the church) and a consumer class (the Christians). Any first-year seminary student can tell you that the church is the people and not the building. Have the people of God been divided between those who provide services and those who pay to have them provided? Absolutely! May God have mercy on us all!

If the church consists of all those who have believed in Jesus, then church leaders must be less concerned with attracting a bigger flock and more concerned with getting the flock out of the pen. The church is presently sitting on the greatest source of power the world has ever known, the Spirit-filled follower of Jesus. When a believer in Christ becomes a follower of Christ, that life and the lives of countless others who will be touched by that life will forever be changed. Every believer sitting in a church week after week enjoying the show is indwelt by the Holy Spirit of God. Imagine what could happen if that same believer stopped just enjoying the show and began to see himself or herself as chosen by God and filled with the power of God so that that same God could use that believer to bring light and life to a dark and dying world. The possible impact is immeasurable!

So how do we start to make the shift from purveyor of spiritual goods and services to enabler of those who are meant to change the world? We must begin by replacing our vision of the church as a business with one of the church as a living entity indwelt and empowered by Almighty God and every believer as the "workmanship of God, created in Christ Jesus for good works which He prepared beforehand for us to do" (Eph. 2:10). This paradigm shift is essential to the transfusion process, but the old paradigm is deeply ingrained. We must completely rethink the way we've understood and experienced church if we are to release believers to reach their full God-given potential.

We've found the concept of DNA helpful in understanding what really makes a church a church. Every living thing has a DNA that defines its unique characteristics. It is present in every cell and determines the size, shape, makeup, and functions of each cell and the organism as a whole. Because the church is alive through the Spirit of God, it, too, we believe, has a DNA.

The DNA of the church consists of *divine truth, nurturing relationships,* and *apostolic mission.* We believe that every member of the body of Christ and every grouping within the church should possess this DNA.

The *D* in DNA stands for Divine Truth. When we talk of divine truth, we are referring to the Word of God, both written and personal. The written word is useful for teaching, reproof, correction, and training in righteousness, "so that the man of God may be adequate, equipped for every good work." But the Word is also personal. Jesus told the Pharisees, "You search the Scriptures because you think that in them you have eternal life, but it's these that testify of Me." And again, "I am the Way, the Truth, and the Life." And again, "I am with you always, even to the end of the age." Any expression of church that doesn't include an awareness of the actual presence of God is missing the main point. Jesus is the Word, the Head of the church, and He is always present. Ensuring that each part of the body is connected to the Head and surrendered to His leading is absolutely necessary for the church (as well as each individual believer) to function as it should. Jesus is not an absentee king who has delegated the task of leading His church to a small committee of Christian leaders while He is away on vacation. He is the king reigning now. He is capable and willing and has been given all the authority necessary to lead His church. He is the Head, and the body must be connected to and listening to Him. As the human body is animated by the human spirit, so the body of Christ is animated by the Spirit of God.

The *N* in DNA stands for nurturing relationships. The church is not called to be a business, a hospital, or a school; it is called to be a family. Intimate personal relationships are necessary for the growth of the body in love. The Scriptures are filled with admonitions that can only be carried out in relationships. Instructions like "through love serve one another," "bear one another's burdens," and "stimulate one another to love and good deeds" illustrate the point. The disciple of Christ must be in close relationship with other disciples of Christ.

In addition to this, there is the principle that iron sharpens iron. If the Spirit of God is present and active in the life of every believer, then God can use any believer to influence or direct another believer or group of believers. This is why the Scriptures say not to despise any prophetic utterance but to examine everything carefully, holding fast to what is good and abstaining from what is evil. It is the responsibility of each and every disciple to listen carefully to everything and determine, with the help of the Spirit, which messages are from God and applicable to the disciple's life.

The *A* in DNA represents apostolic mission. The word *apostle* literally means "sent one." The church (as well as the individual believer) is not meant to be a sending organization but a sent people. God is the sender and we are the sent. "Each one has been given the manifestation of the Spirit for the common good" and "as each one has received a special gift, employ it in serving one another as good stewards of the manifold grace of God." Every believer and therefore every church is filled with people who have been gifted and called by God to fulfill a purpose in this world. For a believer to become a mature disciple, he or she must be given the freedom to follow Christ wherever He leads. After all, they are "His workmanship, created in Christ Jesus for good works which He prepared beforehand for them to do." When a church begins to understand this principle, it will continually be looking to support, prepare, encourage, and release disciples into the purposes for which they were created.

For many churches, this amazing power is present but somehow trapped in the pews. How does leadership go about releasing those pew-padded people to lives of effectiveness in the kingdom of God? That's what the rest of this book attempts to relay.

If you're looking for a quick fix or a step-by-step plan, you won't find it here. But if you are looking for rhythms of life and leadership that will bring lasting effectiveness, you're reading the right book.

The DNA at the core of every disciple, church, network, and global movement is the glue that links us all together and connects us to Jesus, the Head (D), to one another as family members (N), and to the world where we are all on mission (A).

Jesus also emphasized the concepts embodied by our DNA. The greatest commandment is to "love the Lord your God with all your heart, mind, soul, and strength." This is our connection with divine truth. The second greatest is to love your neighbor as yourself, which is the essence of nurturing relationships. Finally, the Great Commission is to go into all the nations and make disciples, which is, of course, apostolic mission.

This DNA is not something new, of course; it is as ancient as the Bible. It is also not uncommon to find many churches and ministries emphasizing the same three components, which should not be a surprise if we are all reading the same Bible. For example, Ed Stetzer and Thom Rainer, in their book *Transformational Church,* use the terms *worship, community,* and *mission* to describe what they call the essential foundations of discipleship.[2] Worship is connecting with the divine truth, community is connecting with others in nurturing relationship, and mission is apostolic mission. Rick Warren refers to the Great Commandment (love God and love others) and the Great Commission (make disciples) to articulate the same three ideas.[3]

While it is not rare to see the same core components emphasized by the church, what is indeed rare is to find all three components functioning holistically within all the disciples of these churches. Most church development resources will carve priorities and practices into these three categories and attempt to implement programs designed to better connect people to each of them.

The problem is that this is not how DNA works. The whole DNA is found in every cell, and the activity flows out from it, not to it. We cannot program DNA from the top down; it must be in the center of every disciple and flow out from there. That is organic growth as opposed to institutional growth.

What is also rare these days is to find people actually trusting in the DNA for the formation and organization of the church. People organize the church according to the DNA rather than allowing the DNA to organize the church, and there is a difference. We must let the DNA do what it alone is meant to do. We say we believe in these three dynamic principles, but at the end of the day, we trust in our own organizational skills and programs more than the DNA itself.

At CMA the initial team of leaders started out with a global movement in mind. Because of this, we made conscious decisions all along our path not to centralize or create an artificial glue to keep us together as an organization. We decided that if the divine truth of Jesus and His Word, the nurturing relationships of being in His family, and the apostolic mission He has given to each of us is not enough to bind us together, than we will not be together.

We purposely chose not to resort to what we saw as lesser forms of organizational glue, such as a single name or brand, organizational dues or covenants, or some other mandated methodology. We determined that Christ as Head and the resulting consequence of our being a family together on His mission was enough and that to substitute something less would eventually kill the movement. With this decision, we lost all sense of control, tracking, and centralized support structure. We often explain to people that we could not possibly count all the churches in CMA, which is true. But actually, we do prefer it this way as well. In this movement we sought to see that Jesus really is enough, and that was worth it to us. We are still in the midst of this grand experiment, and so far He has not disappointed us.

There is a real—though mystical—glue that connects us all in the one body of Christ. "There is one body and one Spirit, just as also you were called in one hope of your calling; one Lord, one faith, one baptism, one God and Father of all who is over all and through all and in all" (Eph. 4:4–6). We are all connected. Part of the problem in our churches is that we believe less in this mystical reality than in our own ability to manipulate and manage outcomes.

We at CMA have chosen to let the presence of God among us be the only glue that binds us together as a movement. Though we do pass on simple reproducible systems that tend to catalyze the formation of disciples, leaders, churches, and movements, the heart of each system is this same DNA, and nothing else is demanded from each disciple, church, or network. None of our systems are mandatory; they are presented as one way of doing the work, a very productive and simple way, but an optional way nonetheless. We understand that mandated methods are not compatible with a decentralized grassroots movement that continually reproduces. Those out in the fields must simply maintain a level of autonomy that allows them to hear from God and decide what He wants them to do in their specific context.

We believe you will find that this DNA is the most important part of everything we say or do. Every one of our books, our trainings, and all our methodologies rise or fall based on this DNA. In fact, as you read further, you will find that this DNA is the key to everything.

We need to make a couple of quick points here that we will fully develop later. It isn't necessary to destroy what currently exists to bring positive change to a church. In the parable of the wineskins, Jesus makes the point that the fermentation of new wine can burst old wineskins. Is He concerned about the wineskins or the wine that they contain? Many church leaders think they must destroy what they have in order to build something new. When they take this tack, they often underestimate the damage that is done to the lives God has already redeemed. Much can be accomplished by creating new wineskins and allowing them to coexist with the old. Wine is meant to be spent, not kept forever. Once the wine is gone the old skins are to be tossed aside. The value is in the wine, not the skins. Life never comes from structure. If we never create new wineskins for the fresh wine we will eventually run out of the wine. Old wine is valuable, and Jesus never wants to spill a drop, but without creating new wine there will never be old wine in the future. It's the wine (those redeemed lives that are filled with the Spirit of God) that is valuable to God and has the power to change the world.

We should recognize that positive change is likely to start small and take some time to permeate the church. "A little leaven leavens the whole lump." Begin by working with people who are ready and willing to take up their cross and follow Jesus. Help them see their potential, and release them to the service of their King. Over time, a culture counter to the one present in your church will begin to emerge and put positive pressure on the rest to change too.

The truth is, your church is only as good as its disciples. We have found that if you are not able to reproduce healthy disciples, you will not be able to reproduce healthy leaders or churches, and there will not be any apostolic movement. It is time for us to lower the bar on how church is done so that anyone can do it and raise the bar on what it means to be a disciple so that all will do it.

In this book we will give examples of how change starts small and then spreads, and we will give instruction for how to catalyze such change. It starts small, as small as a mustard seed, but through reproduction it will bear an abundance of fruit that will have visible effects on the world we live in.

CHAPTER THREE

NO LONGER BUSINESS AS USUAL

Five men sat around a table talking late into the night about the name of our church. Would we remain Grace Brethren Church or become Grace Fellowship? It isn't that big of a difference now as I look back, but in the moment it seemed so important.

This was in the mid-1990s in a suburb outside the Los Angeles area. The five consisted of three young men in their early thirties, including myself (Neil), and two middle-aged men that were actually fathers of the other two younger guys. I remember we had heated discussions on our elder board. I was the pastor of this more established congregational church, and I wanted to bring change. We were thinking that if we changed our name, got a fresh logo, and cast a bigger vision, the church would become healthier and more attractive and would grow. We wanted a new identity in the community. One elder opposed this thought, but we wouldn't let him stop us. We pushed this new vision through, and the elder later excused himself from our leadership team and the church, but we got what we wanted. We changed the name, the logo, the vision—but not the church.

Years later, I have a different view of what brings change to a church. My new view is born from much more experience and admittedly many mistakes. I don't think an established church needs a transition to be healthy and vital. What is truly needed is more than a transition; it needs a *transfusion* of healthy DNA found in the blood of Jesus and nothing less.

Someone once described changing a church's name, structure, or programs to fix the problems it faces as much like rearranging the deck chairs on the *Titanic*—futile and meaningless in altering the outcome.

Church is not an organization or an institution but an organism, a living body. An organization can transition. An organism grows, matures, reproduces, and dies. The thought that we can fix a church by hiring a new staff member or plugging in a new program is ridiculous. Simply changing direction with clever goals and a capital giving campaign is not going to transform a congregation but merely send the same ailing church down a new path.

Many pastors think, "If only we could get a new building or hire another staff member, all would be well. If the music was done better or a slick new sign was outside our building, people would suddenly want to come check us out, and we'd grow."

Most steps taken to change a congregation are really just about polishing up the external appearance; all the while, the body suffers from an internal anemia of sorts. When your body is sick, getting a nice haircut, a new wardrobe, and plastic surgery will only make the job of the undertaker a little easier. If the pastor goes away on a retreat and returns with some new BHAG—a Big Hairy (or "Holy" for us Christians) Audacious Goal[1] for the church to pursue, it will not address the internal health. It is like a sick body turning and choosing to walk up a steep hill; the body is still sick, and the new labored direction will only add more strain.

Solutions to church health are far more internal and serious than a facelift or new ambitious plan can address. If you receive a diagnosis for a serious disorder, a new gym membership is not likely to be the solution. Of course a gym membership is a good thing, but it is not going to cure cancer or diabetes. It can help you become stronger as you face those things, but you need more than a workout to address internal disease.

A growing number of books on how to bring change to a church are available. Most approach the subject from a business or organizational perspective, which we believe is a mistaken approach. Part of the health problem most churches face is that they are built and managed more like a business than a body, so addressing the needed change using the same sort of thinking that caused the problem in the first place is not a true solution.

Rather than learning from business or academia, perhaps we should turn to medicine or agriculture.

TRANSFUSIONAL CHURCHES

There are many traditional expressions of church in the United States that are attempting to transition toward being more organic. Instead of calling them transitional churches, we call them "transfusional churches." The reason for this change is that the idea of transitioning implies simply modifying a model or a system, and we have found that this would be useless without a transfusion of healthy DNA.

Some people suggest that you assess your church's strengths and weaknesses and then work on getting better at things you are not as strong at. Usually there are between seven and eleven healthy indicators that must be addressed in this manner, which are always randomly selected by some author based on current church practices and traditions. This is like evaluating a body and then realizing that your upper body muscles are strong but you lack stamina and your lungs are not working properly because you've been smoking. As a solution, you decide to quit smoking and start running, which is a good idea. The problem, however, is that your DNA has caused you to inherit sickle cell anemia. Working out will not make your body healthier because the problem isn't with your muscles or your lung capacity alone; it is cellular and is actually found in the DNA of every cell in your body. You need a cure that changes every cell of your body.

The problems our churches face in the West are not structural, strategic, or mechanical. A mechanical fix is not a fix at all. The problem is a lack of life in the core, or perhaps a more diplomatic way to describe it is a lack of healthy DNA. So every transformation begins not with a structural change but with a transfusion of holistic and healthy disciples infused with the DNA. We want to see each one fruitful and multiplying enough that there is a vast improvement in the health of the entire church body. Rather than simply use up those disciples in meeting existing ministry needs, we challenge church leadership to release some of them to start groups, perhaps even outside the walls of the congregation itself.

Think for a moment about the importance of DNA. When we speak, we sometimes ask if anyone in the audience would be willing to show us his or her DNA. Usually people laugh at the thought and someone eventually stands up with arms extended and says, "Here it is." You see, the whole DNA is in every cell of your body.[2] The code that causes the cells of your eyes to see or your brain to think is also found in equal proportion in your big toe or your pinkie. Why? Your big toe doesn't need to see or think, but the entire DNA is there just as it is in your eye or brain.

If your DNA were somehow corrupted with a mutation, how would you fix it? You can't conduct surgery on every cell of your body. You can't just take a pill and hope that that will fix things. The healthy DNA must infiltrate every cell for the body to become healthy, and in the same way, every disciple in the church must have the complete DNA within if we hope to resurrect the body to become a healthy organic church.

Change DNA?

Changing your church's model or mechanical structure is like trying to take a pill to fix your DNA. It can't be done. The problem is not something that the leaders can fix alone because the problem is found in every cell or person in the body of Christ.

Of course, in today's world changing someone's DNA is merely science fiction. We cannot fix a person with Down syndrome by medical means. Maybe someday this will be possible, but today it is fiction. But then again, the idea of resurrection is also science fiction. Supernatural healing is not possible with science, but we believe it is possible for the Messiah, so perhaps healing one's DNA (or the DNA of a church) is a possibility with Jesus.

But if we could somehow fix someone's DNA, I would imagine we would need a more viral approach that brings change one cell at a time. To do that you would first need to introduce a healthy DNA cell that is capable of reproducing. The change would be microscopic and slow to begin with, but as each generation of transformed cells reproduced, it would build momentum, and change would eventually be noticeable. The same is true for each person who has the DNA of healthy discipleship within the context of an established church body.

Once healthy discipleship is under way, leaders can be trained not to get in the way of the continuing growth in disciples, leaders, churches, and movements. This is not as easy as it sounds because most leaders have been trained to think their input is the most vital ingredient in the process. At CMA we even talk about going through "detox" at this stage, because we have created such a dependence in our churches that people are not self-sufficient or self-replicating. This detox causes death. We must die to our-selves, to our past, and to our future ambitions in order to be born again to a new way of working. We sometimes suggest that churches have an official funeral service in which the leaders go first. Leadership, in one very profound sense, is simply being willing to lead by going first. We need crucified leaders that will demonstrate what it means to die to themselves—their personal ambitions, hopes, dreams, and provisions—and allow Christ to rule in the new reborn life.

At our training events, when a large number of church leaders are present, we will often ask the pastors to figuratively hand the keys to the church they lead over to Jesus and repent of taking ownership and direction away from the true Head of the church. Jesus said, "*I* will build *My* church" (Matt. 16:18). It's not your church, pastor; it never was. The people are not your people. And most important, it is not your reputation that is at stake with the church's success or failure; it's God's.

After the pastor has died to himself or herself and given the church back to Jesus, we recommend that the church also have a memorial service. What would a church memorial service look like? Why not gather around a gravesite for the church, if nothing else a hole in the ground with a wood box filled with something representing the church. Perhaps each of the mourners gets to share a story of how the church affected his or her life. Afterward the pastor prays and lays the church to rest in the symbolic wood box. The mourners throw a handful of dirt on top as they each lay aside their own personal investment in the church so that they no longer have a stake in the church's success or failures. In the end, the old church has died and a new one can be born. Every-one can have a sense of anticipation of what God may birth. (It is also a good indicator of the willingness of people to change.)

Perhaps the next week you can have a baby shower for the newly born-again church and everyone can bring a new symbolic gift. Many churches have a cornerstone that dates the construction of the building; why not have a symbolic plaque or stone that represents the church's death and resurrection as well? This could be something to remind the congregants every time they walk past that they have died to their old ways of being a church and been reborn to become the church Jesus desires. The point of these symbolic exercises is for the people to surrender the church to God's new will rather than remain stuck in an old pattern. With good teaching in advance we believe that many congregations will be open to such a practice. We will further examine this idea and many of its implications for a church in Chapter Five. Lest you think this too harsh, realize that this is the entrance requirement Jesus demands of any who would follow Him.

Phil Helfer, my coauthor and an original founder of CMA, is actually the most radical organic thinker on our team. I have learned much from him. But Phil leads Los Altos Grace Brethren Church in Long Beach, California, a church that is more than fifty years old at a facility that has age-graded Sunday school classes and a preschool through sixth-grade school on campus. It averages three hundred to four hundred people in attendance weekly. This does not look or feel at all like an organic church, but it is transfusional. Slowly Phil has been training his leaders to think and respond more organically using the ideas shared throughout this book. His leadership team has bought into organic values and habitually practices them.

When we speak of organic values or thinking, we are talking about those things that produce and sustain life. Because the church is a living thing, its leaders must lead from a set of values that are fundamentally different from those used in the business world. What Phil has done is create an atmosphere where the first question leaders ask is "How will this affect the life and health of Christ's body and enable all members to play the part God has for them?" This way of thinking causes the leaders to be vastly more focused on the needs and development of each disciple than they would otherwise be.

As a result, this church sent me and my family out to start Awakening Chapels, our first organic church network in what is today a rapidly expanding movement around the world. It also launched three other organic church networks and several single-house churches that have yet to become networks. Although a church like Phil's is not likely to start spontaneously reproducing anytime soon, it can become a grandparent to movements by releasing disciples to start networks that look quite different.

Today many churches are seriously looking at ways to become more like organic networks than centralized congregations. We are in constant conversations with several megachurches, well known for their strong and dynamic leadership, that are asking how they can change and multiply.

REIMAGINING CHURCH

Recently I (Neil) was asked what I think about the upswing in the trend of church mergers. I first responded with a question of my own: do you want the real answer or the nice one? To the questioner's credit, he asked for the real one, and I gave it.

Merger is a business term that applies when two separate corporations consolidate all their assets to form one single and larger organization. Usually this strategy is driven by greed—for money, influence, and greater control of a market.

Talk of merger is actually a symptom of a very serious affliction in the kingdom of God: the view of church as a business. The thinking behind a merger is that the church is a business with assets, employees, a board of directors, and a product it offers to its customers. Many of you are probably nodding in agreement that this is an accurate description of what your church is today. Friends, that is how far removed we are from the New Testament.

Delving further into a false paradigm in an attempt to do it better is a bad idea. Why would you want to be better at doing something wrong? Yet we believe that many of the new trends in church are just that. Franchising your church brand via multisite is a similar idea. (We just offended a bunch of our friends, didn't we?)

But seriously, the idea of multisite is that we have a single church that meets in different locations. Some observers claim that this is very much like the New Testament. Perhaps, but in fact that is true of the body of Christ in general, isn't it? "One body—one Lord, one faith, one baptism . . . "

But multisite is more than this. It puts a single brand on a church, usually tied to a dynamic teacher or perhaps a methodology, and appeals to Christians as consumers looking for that brand of service. Sometimes the sites offer the same preacher but a different style of music in order to appeal to a variety of consumers. This again is a symptom of a bigger problem with our view of church. The church is not a business. It is a living entity. It is the body of Christ animated by the Spirit of God.

Leaders lose sight of its character and mission when they use business practices to organize and operate it. The church was never meant to be operated. It is meant to be cared for. In many ways this approach in a single church is a microcosm of denominationalism, which brands a certain form of church and functions as a corporation. Of course, denominationalism is not biblical either. Wherever competition exists for a market share, we are doing business for ourselves and not the work of the kingdom. We are afraid that much of what is taking place in the church today is more of the latter than the former.

What I said in response to the question about church mergers was that church is not a business, nor is it a building. It's not a weekly event to attend, and it's not just an organization or corporation.

In the Bible, the church is not defined but instead is described with similes: a flock, a field, a family, a body, a bride, a branch, a building made of living stones. Never is it described by the images we typically have today: a building, a business, a school, or a hospital. We have replaced an organic and life-producing view with an institutional one that does not produce life and at best simply tries to preserve it and contain it.

Jesus faced this same problem. Let's look at his response to a similar situation when business practices had invaded the household of God. Mark 11:15–18 reads:

> Then they came to Jerusalem. And He entered the temple and began to drive out those who were buying and selling in the temple, and overturned the tables of the money changers and the seats of those who were selling doves; and He would not permit anyone to carry merchandise through the temple. And He began to teach and say to them, "Is it not written, 'My house shall be called a house of

prayer for all the nations'? But you have made it a robbers' den." The chief priests and the scribes heard this, and began seeking how to destroy Him; for they were afraid of Him, for the whole crowd was astonished at His teaching.

Examining this passage, my good friend and ministry cola- borer Paul Kaak suggests we ask, "Why were they so fearful and so murderously angry?" Paul points out that Jesus' words were a double-edged indictment. The people had substituted their true calling for a false identity. They had become distributors of reli- gious goods and services and had abandoned their true missional identity, becoming takers rather than givers. Rather than propa- gating the freedom of truth to all people without prejudice, they were now focused on preserving the institution, financially and culturally, at all costs. They became a religious business that needed to be maintained rather than a missional spiritual family. Does that sound familiar?

We must be careful to not do the same thing. The church today generally contains, conforms, and controls the believers in its care. The biblical pictures of the New Testament are all about releasing and reproducing the life of the church, not managing and controlling financial or other interests.

Inorganic things can produce but not reproduce. As Christian Schwartz points out so eloquently, "A coffee maker can make coffee (praise God), but it cannot make more coffee makers."[3] Jesus intends for his bride and body to be fertile and for his branches to bear fruit. Jesus didn't use images of an institution when describing His church, nor should we.

Jesus has great patience and shows much grace. God's patience is often called long-suffering because, frankly, His patience leads Him to suffer long. We believe there is hope for our churches today. We are not suggesting that the vast majority of churches today are all wrong and need to shut down. We are simply stating that we need to stop seeing church through faulty lenses that ultimately corrupt our church practices and establish jaded views of success. Let's stop functioning like a business and start relating to one another like a body. Let's move beyond being an academic insti- tution and start becoming a disciple-making and reproducing movement. Let's start seeing church as a family on mission together rather than a once-a-week religious event to make each of us feel better for the week ahead.

Facing a corrupt and self-benefiting system, Jesus addressed the problem forcefully by calling it out. He sharply contrasts what is in Scripture verses and what they were teaching and doing by saying, "Is it not written . . . but you have . . . " If we wake up one day and find that our current practices are not based on what is written in the Scriptures but are in fact opposing them, we need to abandon those practices in favor of the truth of God's Word, no matter how painful that may be.

It is also important to note that in Jesus' passionate words about the household of God, he emphasizes what is truly most important: the DNA. He says, "My house shall be called a house (*relational family—nurturing relationship*) of prayer (*connecting with divine truth*) for all the nations (*apostolic mission*)."

Frankly, it is time that we put an abrupt end to the business model of church and get back to a real focus on the true DNA of the body of Christ. We should address this with the same sense of urgency Jesus exhibited on that day in the Temple.

THE CHALLENGES OF CHANGE

Transforming the culture of a church is a tremendous challenge. When one looks at the entirety of the church, it is easy to become overwhelmed and not know where even to start. Many people have chosen to resign and start something new because of this, but some do not have that option. If your calling is to transfuse an established church, there are many areas you will need to address, and we will look at a number of these in more detail in the chapters that follow.

○ *The Core: Integrating the DNA into the life of the individual disciple instead of finding it in an agenda, curriculum, program, ministry style or leader's personality.* If you are wondering where to start, this is it. If you skip this, then everything else will likely be in vain. If you accomplish this correctly, everything else that needs to be done may simply follow. The health that reproduces must be found within and cannot be put in from the outside.

○ *The Flow: Switching from a centripetal force sucking inward to a centrifugal force sending out.* Transfusing a church takes as much energy as changing the course of a river. It's in fact a very different kind of energy. Instead of centripetal force, whereby the energy pulls something inward, like the water swirling around the bathtub drain, you are changing it to centrifugal force, whereby the energy pulls outward and away, as on a potter's wheel. If your church is successful at attracting people, you will face the task of switching the flow of energy from coming in to sending people out into their workplaces and neighborhoods. You cannot suck in water and spit it out at the same time.

If a church has been built on attracting people to attend a worship service, this change to an outward orientation will be challenging. In a sense you have nonverbally told people that church is for them and they have come believing that it will provide them with spiritual nourishment in exchange for regular attendance and a tithe or offering. To now get them to see that they are for the church *and* the world almost comes across as a bait-and-switch ploy, but the change must be made. This is the challenge that you face.

○ *The Standard: Measuring influence of people multiplied to several generations, not numbers of people attending a program.* In the old system it was easy to tell if you were successful or not; you simply counted the attenders and the dollars. The organic way of measuring success is not nearly so easy. Having lots of people is not as much a measure of success as having people of influence making a difference in the world.

○ *The Environment: Changing from a very controlled environment to an uncontrolled and spontaneous one.* In a sense the thing that got you "success" in the old system will be the very thing that will prevent success in the new one. In a highly attractional church system, quality is what is most important, and higher quality requires a higher degree of control and expertise. Unfortunately, control and specialized ministry implemented by experts are two things that work directly against an organic movement.

There is no human control over an organic multiplication movement, and even the hint of control will bring any movement to a grinding halt. The reasons for this are many. Here are a few: (1) The growth, direction, and order of the church in movement come from the presence of Christ and His DNA within, not from outside engineering. (2) Within the very definition of a multiplication movement is the essential idea that each generation reproduces itself. Once you multiply to the third and fourth generation and beyond, you will quickly realize that any idea of controlling the movement is pure fiction. (3) Perhaps the primary reason why control is not possible in a multiplication movement is that God is placed in charge from the start, and if we wrestle the control back to ourselves, we will sabotage the movement immediately.

The real question is, Why would we want control? Do we really think we can produce something better than God can? Roland Allen in his classic book *The Spontaneous Expansion of the Church and the Causes That Hinder It* remarks:

> By spontaneous expansion I mean something which we cannot control. . . . The great things of God are beyond our control. Therein lies a vast hope. Spontaneous expansion could fill the continents with the knowledge of Christ: our control cannot reach as far as that. We constantly bewail our limitations: open doors unentered; doors closed to us as foreign missionaries; fields white to the harvest, which we cannot reap. Spontaneous expansion could enter open doors, force closed ones, and reap those white fields. Our control cannot: it can only appeal pitifully for more men to maintain control.[4]

For spontaneous life and reproduction to occur, spontaneity must be encouraged. If every second of time together is scheduled, planned, and managed, you will never see spontaneous multiplication. I have been to many church gatherings where every millisecond of the time is planned and rehearsed. There is no room for spontaneity in this scenario; there is no time to let God do what only He can do. Control and spontaneity are two completely different things; trying to get spontaneous results from a controlled environment is like trying to get fire from ice.

○ *The Instigators: Transitioning from specialized experts to general equippers.* In an organic movement, everyone, not just highly trained specialists, is crucial to carrying the movement. The kind of leadership that works in movements will be found not doing ministry but equipping others to do it. Leaders are not called to the ministry, as we so often say, but called to get others to do the ministry. And they are not called to get others to do the ministry they prescribe but the one to which they are uniquely called. Leaders must lead people to a place where they are willing to surrender themselves to the will of God for life. It is from this place of surrender and dependence that true ministry is accomplished. Apostles, prophets, evangelists, shepherds, and teachers are to equip the saints to do the work of ministry, not to do it for them.[5]

TRANSITIONS

Ed Stetzer and David Putman, in their book *Breaking the Missional Code,* have a chapter about shifting to missional ministry in which they describe ten transitions that must be worked out.[6] These are a good overview of how much a church must change to become effective, fruitful, and organic in its ministry. These are the ten transitions:

1. From Programs to Processes
2. From Demographics to Discernment
3. From Models to Missions
4. From Attractional to Incarnational
5. From Uniformity to Diversity
6. From Professional to Passionate
7. From Seating to Sending
8. From Decisions to Disciples
9. From Additional to Exponential
10. From Monuments to Movements

Exhibit 2.1 describes the contrast between a transitional approach to church change verses a transfusional approach.

Exhibit 2.1 Contrasts Between Transitional and Transfusional Approaches

	Transitional	Transfusional
Desired Outcome:	Get people in	Get people out
Measure of Success:	Institutional (numbers)	Influential (stories)
Uniting Factor:	External branding	Internal DNA
Decision Making:	From the top	From the grassroots
Leadership:	Specialized ministers	Generalized equippers
Growth:	Addition	Multiplication
Growth Focus:	Recruit more leaders	Raise better disciples
Environment:	Controlled	Spontaneous
Organization:	More centralized	More decentralized
Point of influence:	The meeting place	The marketplace

Easing the Transfusion

Some denominations and governance systems are easier to transfuse than others; it would be irresponsible to tell you otherwise. Not all churches and denominations have equal opportunities in this process. Though we believe that the processes of change are universal and available for all, the starting place makes a huge difference. Following are some of the things we have found that make for an easier transfusion.

The younger the church, the easier it is to transfuse. A new church plant has fewer institutionalized qualities that must be undone. Every year that passes sets more of the culture in stone and makes for a more difficult change.

The more desperate the church, the easier it is to transfuse. On the other side of the coin, the more desperate a church is, the more likely it will be willing to pay the price that is required for change. A church's decline and death do not usually appear as a slow, steady drop but often mirror the same exponential curve that is seen in rapid growth and multiplication, only in the wrong direction. In other words, once a church starts a downward decline in health, that decline will proceed more and more rapidly with each season that passes. At first, people may still be hopeful of straightening things out because the drop starts off gradually. As the drop increases in steepness, a sense of desperation begins to set in. This can be very useful in motivating change. So perhaps your church is not a new one but very old and very far down the steep slope of decline; that too is a good context from which to instigate transfusion.

Less of a clergy dogma makes for an easier time with transfusion. Some denominations have a very elaborate dogma around the establishment of clergy. The call and ordination of leadership can become a grand and highly valued doctrine that often carries the supposed authority of Scripture behind it, even though the Bible says nothing of clergy. Some of the more reformed traditions require a master's degree from a specific academic institution just to be eligible to lead a church.

Usually, in such an environment, the functions of leadership are also very restrictive. Only ordained clergy are allowed to share communion or baptize new disciples. All of these things will make transfusion a greater challenge. If you find yourself in such a denomination, the good news is that the processes for change are still the same and still possible, but you will likely need to let things work well below the radar for a time. You may also have to be content with less recognized value within your denomination for a while. Our experience is that when people start coming to Christ and transformation is evident, the denominational leadership will be far more tolerant of the differences. Unfortunately, that also makes the newly effective ministry of which you are part an attractive target for institutional leaders. They may try to get their hands on the work in order to "legitimize" it or to stop it. Either can become lethal to birthing movements.

The churches where the senior leadership desires the transfusion will be more likely to succeed. Senior leadership is not necessary to birth a movement outside of an established church, but to birth a transfusion within a church culture it is. This is because the church environment usually highly values the senior leadership and will not bypass it. That said, for some churches the reality is not always that the senior pastor is the senior leadership. There are a great many congregationally run churches that seem to have a new pastor every other year. In those cases the senior pastor usually does not carry the voice of authority, which is found instead in a few trustees on the elder or deacon board. In either case, if the senior leadership—pastoral staff or volunteer board—does not buy in to the transfusion, none will likely occur. It is not the ideal environment, but it is a reality nonetheless, and if the "gatekeepers" of the church close the door on transfusion, the best you can hope for is to birth something new out of it.

The less program-intensive your ministry, the easier the transfusion will be. Many churches have invested everything into programs that they believe will result in the spiritual growth and maturity of their people. Unfortunately, this is a bankrupt system with misplaced faith. Not that every program is wrong and doomed to failure, but involvement in programs is not what brings about sanctification. The more the people of your church are busy with programs, the less they will be free to invest in the relationships and mission that are necessary for the transfusion of DNA. A highly active but relationally poor church is going to struggle in transfusion.

The less your church is built on consumer-driven ideas, the easier your transfusion process will be. If your church has grown quickly because of high-quality performances in weekend services, it may actually be harder to transfuse. Because you have drawn people with a high-powered performance, releasing them back into the world feels a lot like the bait-and-switch we mentioned earlier. The more successful you have been at this, the more the people within the church will feel that they are doing things right and even the hint of change will be met with ambivalence. What you used to attain one sort of success is the very thing that will stand in the way of another form of success. If your church is large and growing because of these things, the people you have are still there because they like what you are doing. One of our sayings is "What you win them with is what you win them to." Your success can become a liability, your strength a weakness.

A church with new Christians will transfuse more easily than one with more mature Christians. Whenever a church is growing because of evangelism, there is an opportunity to birth something new within the hearts of the new followers. It does not take long, however, for a new believer to become infected with the status quo of conventional Churchianity. New Christians will almost always defer decision making and values to the older Christians in a group. If the older Christians have all become sterile in their spiritual life and are no longer reaching out to pockets of lost people, it will not take very long for the new Christians to catch this contagious apathy and become just like the rest. For this reason, the churches that have a strong outreach and regularly pump new followers into the mix will find transfusion an easier process.

THE TRANSFUSION PROCESS

Throughout the second part of this book we will elaborate on the things we find necessary to bring organic transfusion to a church. Here we will simply present a general overall process for you to think through. We are not presenting a formal five-step plan. It is simply a bird's-eye view of the process of transfusion. To bring transfusion to a church body, we suggest that you follow this simple progressive pattern.[7]

1. *See it.* Change agents and innovators must see the potential of a transfused church. They must understand and envision an organic body functioning in complete connection with the Head.
2. *Want it.* If there is going to be a contagion of health within the body, then those who would spread the healthy DNA must want it badly enough to endure the process necessary to bring complete change to a congregation. It must be birthed first as a passion in the leader's own heart before it becomes transfusion in the leader's church.
3. *Pray for it.* The passion for this change needs to be such that it often becomes the subject of your prayers. "Prayer," as

someone once said, "is the slender nerve that moves the muscle of omnipotence." If you want it badly enough, you will pray for it passionately. If you find you haven't been praying for it, perhaps that means you don't really want it badly enough yet.

4. *Pay for it.* There is a cost to change, and not to tell you this up front would be misleading. If a fully functioning body, with each part connected to the Head and reaching out into the world with the transformative gospel, is indeed worthwhile, you will pay the price necessary to see it happen. People who are comfortable with the way things have been will resist the changes. Doing church organically may mean less financial security for leadership. Leaders who have developed a reputation for their expertise may find that the new changes mean that their importance is lessened as they must become equippers of others rather than specialized leaders on which the church depends. These are but a few of the costs that some will have to face. Count the cost up front, which is what Jesus taught; then if it is worth it, pay for it.

5. *Do it.* Make it happen. It will come about in phases, not all at once. It will start small and slow, but if things are done right, it will increase in speed and breadth of transformation over time. You must first live as a connected member of Christ's body before you can ask others to do the same. Personal transformation precedes community transformation. Live it out yourself first.

As we said, these are not five formal steps to transfusion but more a general overview of the process. This book is not ordered after this pattern, but you will find each of the steps discussed in places throughout the book.

It may help to see this played out in other churches as examples. Chapter Four will help you picture what transfusion has looked like in five very different kinds of churches. What happens in your church will be unique. You cannot simply mimic what we describe in Chapter Four, but you can take courage as you watch how organic life is transforming these churches.

CHAPTER FOUR

CHURCHES IN TRANSFUSION

Although CMA has been starting new churches and networks in an expanding movement over the past fifteen years, several established churches have been experiencing a transfusion of the organic way of life and faith as well. In this chapter we will set out to describe five of these churches and how they were transfused.

You will notice immediately that these churches are all very different from one another, so this is not about a model of church or simply plugging in a new program. We realize from these examples that all sorts of churches can experience this transfusion and bear fruit from organic life. There are, however, some common lessons that each has learned that hint at some universal principles that must be a part of a transfusion process. In this chapter we will describe the transfusion process of each of these churches. In future chapters we will go into detail about these more universal principles of transfusion churches.

VINEYARD CENTRAL, CINCINNATI, OHIO

Vineyard Central was a typical Vineyard church plant, meeting in a community center. On a Friday, the city officials informed the pastor, Dave Nixon, that the following Sunday would be the last one they could use the center. That Sunday, Dave stood up before the congregation and had everyone go to different corners of the room. Those who lived on the north side of town were to go to one corner, south side to another, east and west to opposite corners. They all thought this was going to be some sort of experiential learning time. Instead, Dave informed them that they no longer had a meeting space. "Choose a leader, a leader to be, a home, and someone who can lead worship and someone to love the children," he said. "Look around. This is now your church until you hear from us." Stunned, the people did what he asked, and they were suddenly a network of organic churches.

Actually, it takes a little more to become a network of organic churches. But this was a start. Under the leadership of one young man, Kevin Rains, Dave saw some new life, and a single-house church started not just to grow but multiply. Listening to the leading of the Holy Spirit, Dave felt that Kevin had the right gift mix for this new season of the church, so he asked Kevin to become the point leader, and Dave would support him. Now *that* is a rare hero. Not many pastors in today's church world would have the courage to make such a move. Dave is humble and in touch with the Spirit enough that not only did they make this move, but many years later, they are still working closely together. Dave is the closest example I have seen today of the spirit that Barnabas had.

Some time later, a Roman Catholic church in the center of the community became available, so the congregation began to meet there for Sunday worship again. The Catholic church still owned the building but did not intend to use it and so invited Vineyard Central to make an offer to buy it, which Vineyard did, for $150,000. This actually bought an entire city block, which included a huge cathedral with tall ceilings and stained-glass windows, a two-story education wing, a 5,000-square-foot convent, and an equally large rectory.

With this real estate purchase, Vineyard Central was once again back to the normal church thing, albeit in rather unusual surroundings for a Vineyard church. But the people were changed. They had tasted a more organic expression of life together, and they didn't want to go back to the way things had been. They considered what to do with the property. The building, though beautiful, was old and required a lot of repairs and upkeep. They discussed their options and realized that the stained-glass windows alone were worth more then the whole mortgage. They found a buyer for the windows and then decided to knock down the building and create a park for the community. At the last minute, however, the buyer backed out, and the Lord seemed to say that they should keep the building. It was almost an Abraham and Isaac test: Were they willing to give up the building? They passed the test.

Today they use the building for community events such as art shows and quarterly network meetings of all the churches around the city. They use the convent and rectory for living together in community and holistic mentoring of their leaders that they send out to start new works in other places.

Kevin had still been employed full-time by the church but felt the conviction that he needed to be an ordinary guy like everyone else who led in the church. He decided to give up his salary and go back to work for his dad, who owned an auto body repair shop and wanted to retire. Kevin took over the business. Because of Kevin's apostolic gifting, which tends to be more entrepreneurial and a starter of new things, the shop grew and he started a second one just a few blocks from the church building. This keeps Kevin deeply rooted in the neighborhood that God has called him to. About eighty other people have intentionally relocated to this neighborhood to be an incarnational presence there. Many have purchased homes, and others have started businesses in the neighborhood.

The auto body shops have done well. In a short time due to the success of the auto body shops, not only could Kevin's dad retire, but Kevin began to plan his retirement as well. After he retires from the businesses, he can go back to providing all his time to kingdom work without taxing his network of churches financially. Kevin also started reaching out to the guys at work. They began a church after work called Jesus at the Pub: Kevin would meet with the guys, teach and learn about Jesus and His kingdom, and buy the first round!

Some transfusional observations: We fully understand that very few churches will find themselves as dramatically led into a more organic expression of ministry as Vineyard Central, at least not in the current state of the West. If persecution increases, however, this example may yet prove to be very helpful. Nevertheless, even in today's spiritual climate, there are some important lessons every church can learn from Vineyard Central. First and foremost is that leadership must be listening to God, open to whatever He brings, willing to sacrifice self for the good of the church, and lead by example. Second, the placing of value on relational connectivity over facilities is a clear benchmark of organic transfusion. Finally, this church was willing to take risks for the sake of mission, and there is no other way for a church to truly transfuse.

THE WELL, ORANGE COUNTY, CALIFORNIA

The First Southern Baptist Church of La Habra, California, was started in 1952 and for fifty years experienced the ebbs and flows of ministry. At one time the church had an average attendance of nearly seven hundred, but by late 2003, the numbers had dwindled to fifteen or twenty. Pastors seemed to come and go like there was a revolving door at the back of the sanctuary. The members finally chose to sell their property, bank the money (nearly $1 million), rent a new facility at a storefront in nearby Fullerton, and live off the interest.

This is where Ken Eastburn entered the picture. After being approached to take on this ailing church in its new location, Ken initially declined, but God worked on his heart and he accepted the responsibility. The church decided to change its name to The Well, updated the look, and tried to make the facility as attractive as possible. These changes seemed positive but did not go far enough. The board required that Ken have an altar call at the end of every service even though most of those attending had been saved for years. When Ken tried to change the Wednesday night prayer meeting that no one attended or stop paying for a worship team, he was met with stern opposition. The church was paying nearly $5,000 per month for the facility, but its leaders wouldn't allow the $1 million in the bank to be touched on the premise of saving that for the day they would once again buy property. Without access to the savings, The Well could not continue to afford the rent. Ken began to feel like he "was steering a sinking ship filled with untouchable cargo that would surely capsize sooner or later."

In the summer of 2004, the church's treasurer, Bonnie, approached Ken with an idea. In a sweet and supportive way, she suggested that the church buy a house where Ken and his family could live and the church could meet. The idea sparked something in Ken. He got on the Internet and searched "house" and "church." He was surprised by what he found.

Before him were thousands of articles about doing church in home settings. He says of that moment, "I was immediately obsessed and terrified all at the same time." As Ken digested what he read and talked to people who had been doing church this way, a frightening question was birthed in his heart. "How could I suggest transplanting the entire congregation from the brick and mortar it knew, loved, and clung dearly to?"

In September 2004, Ken and his wife, Ali, his youth pastor, and three other members from the church attended a house church conference in Denver, Colorado. As the conference unfolded, Ken held his breath in fear of what his team's response would be. To his amazement, when the conference concluded, the consensus was "We have to do this."

After much prayer, Ken hesitantly brought the new idea to the board for consideration. He was surprised again. The idea of transitioning toward house churches was met with enthusiasm. Ken says he felt like he had fallen backward into something that was never on his radar. The idea was brought to the rest of the church, and the decision to move forward was made, though not without opposition. There were still some people in the church who thought the plan wouldn't work, and there were many on the outside, especially well-respected pastors and leaders within the denomination, who thought the idea was nuts. Some even complained ignorantly that the concept was "not biblical."

After several months of praying, fasting, and dreaming together, The Well left the rented space behind and began meeting in homes. Ken wondered if he'd done the right thing. He sometimes feared that he had led the church off a cliff, but these doubts and fears were overshadowed by the sense that God was indeed moving them forward. These church members had taken their first steps in a journey toward organic living but were still not fully aware of the magnitude of the paradigm shift that they were experiencing.

In the beginning there were three organic churches, and all of them wanted Ken to be present. Ken agreed, thinking it was probably good to keep an eye on things. But as more house churches started, it became impossible for him to make all the meetings. It was difficult at first hearing how well some of them had gone without him.

As new leaders of new home groups emerged, the need to understand biblical leadership grew. The leaders took time to search the Scriptures together to find these principles and then evaluated each other as to how well they were doing. Their bylaws needed changing, and their goals needed an overhaul. They went about doing these things the same way—with prayer, study, discussion, and mutual agreement.

Ken's role in the church is different now. He no longer spends large amounts of time in sermon preparation or worrying and stressing about how "Sunday morning" will be received. Instead, he spends most of his time meeting with and discipling others. The role of church leadership has changed too. Whereas the focus used to be on making decisions and establishing directives, it now has much more of a family feel. The leaders pray and talk and don't make decisions until they reach consensus.

The Well has come to see itself as a more decentralized expression of church. When the groups meet, they often share a meal and then talk about what God has been doing among them, discuss the Scriptures, and pray for each other and the opportunities God has set before them. They have one expectation of every member: that each of them listens to and obeys God. This has led to a renewed interest in sharing the good news locally and beyond.

The Well emphasizes three "critical catalysts" that must be present in the church: relating personally to God, loving God's people, and being God's representative. Notice the DNA? Divine truth is relating personally to God, nurturing relationship is loving God's people, and apostolic mission is being God's representative. Ken says that living out the precepts of the DNA has infused The Well with the spiritual energy it needs to make steady progress toward becoming like Jesus in this lifetime.

As an example of the kind of fruit The Well has seen, Ken shares the following story.

My wife, Ali, met Jamie at a local women's Bible study. Jamie had come because a neighbor had invited her. Jamie did not claim to be a Christian or really believe in the Bible as God's Word. She came to be polite and possibly to get some ammo against "typical Christians."

Ali and Jamie became friends, and Jamie, a photographer, agreed to take some family pictures for us. My family went to a local park for the photo shoot, and that is where I first met her. Sometime after the shoot, Ali informed Jamie that I was a pastor. "I had no idea," she said. "He doesn't seem like a pastor." I took that as a compliment.

A little time went by, and eventually we invited Jamie and her husband, Josh, over for dinner. Jamie had warned Ali that her husband wanted nothing to do with Jesus or Christians and was pretty "hostile toward the church." I wasn't sure what that meant or what to expect. But it turned out that we had a great time and a very stimulating conversation. Josh is a very passionate person with very strong opinions about the world and even about God. It wasn't that he didn't believe in God, but he had no room in his life for organized religion. The church had wounded him and his family when he was younger. As they were leaving our house, both Josh and Jamie hugged us, and we felt as if we had made new friends.

A couple of weeks after that, we invited Josh and Jamie back for a Sunday morning breakfast. After breakfast they asked a couple of questions about God and asked if we could look up the answers in the Bible. This was completely their idea. After a pretty interesting discussion, they asked if we would come to their house for breakfast the following week to continue the discussion. They had invited another couple, and again, we had a nice meal and another engaging discussion about spiritual things.

They asked if we would consider coming back the following week. We agreed, and little did they realize that a church was being born in their home. Over the next few months, Josh and Jamie began to invite friends and family members to their home for breakfast and a "spiritual discussion." Eventually they began to call it church. That was three years ago. That group of people has gone through a lot together. They are now a community that goes camping together, helps each other when there is financial need, celebrates birthdays and holidays together, and cares about each other. It's just that simple.

By bringing Jesus to the people and allowing the seed of the gospel to grow where it was planted, a new church was born and new people were taught to follow Jesus.

The Well has continued to be shaped by the work and presence of Christ. It has seen many churches started like the one just described. It has also partnered to see organic churches planted in Ghana on the continent of Africa. It has sent people four times to this nation to pass on ideas and see firsthand what God is doing there.

The sacrifice of property for the sake of the kingdom of God did not end with The Well; it only began there. Ali, Ken's wife, was also led by the Spirit to give away her prized wedding ring to aid the poor in Africa. This sacrifice became contagious, and soon others were giving their rings and other possessions to Ali for the cause of digging wells in places where people didn't have adequate drinking water. A nonprofit ministry, called With This Ring, was born organically from The Well.

This church has gone from being self-absorbed and self-concerned, tainted with the smell of impending death, to a church that is full of life and fruitfulness.

Some transfusional observations: As with Vineyard Central, there were outside forces propelling The Well toward change. Finances were tight, and attendance was low. Notice that the change began in Ken's heart first. God was leading him toward something new and life-giving. God also brought other members of The Well to the same conclusions, and as they shared these insights with each other, an excitement was born in them. This excitement led to a contagious hope that transformed the whole church.

Not all churches will be led to take the radical steps of divesting themselves of property, but in this case holding on to it was an obstacle to the church's development. Church members' willingness to let go of the things that were in the way became the seed bed in which God did His work. They changed from being focused on the preservation of a dying organization to being focused on people and the life God could birth and grow in them.

LOS ALTOS GRACE, LONG BEACH, CALIFORNIA

I (Phil) like to refer to Los Altos Grace as a fifty-seven-year-old church plant. It was started as a Christian school in Long Beach,

California, in the early 1950s. It opened one Easter morning and attracted people from the newly built homes that surrounded its property.

From the beginning, this was an ordinary church plant. It offered services to the community such as programs for children and youth, Sunday school for all ages, and an opportunity to worship and learn from the Bible on Sunday mornings. Over the years, church attendance rose and fell, and many pastors came and went. My wife, Lori, was a baby in the nursery at Los Altos. Her parents, Don and Joan, had been part of the church-planting effort and then lifelong members of the congregation. After Lori and I married, and while I was serving as an associate pastor in a small church in Orange County, Los Altos found itself without a pastor once again. My wife and I considered the possibility of stepping forward as candidates but decided against it because of the church's reputation. It had become known as the "pastor killer church." Many pastors had stayed but a short while, and there was a general sense that the church was not happy with any of them. A new pastor was finally found, however, one who had big ideas and a plan for growth. There seemed to be a new wind blowing, and people were excited about the future. We visited the church one Sunday morning so that my wife, who has a beautiful voice, could sing in the Sunday service. We were impressed with the positive spirit that seemed to pervade the place. Things were looking up.

I was between jobs, and we decided to begin attending Los Altos. The church had attracted many young families who were in need of shepherding. Lori and I, along with a few others, began a young married class that met during the Sunday school hour each week. In a short period of time, the class grew considerably, and even though I was not on staff, I found that my responsibilities for nurture and discipleship were growing considerably too.

During the first couple of years I was underemployed and looking for a church to pastor. Every time my wife and I would interview, we couldn't escape the feeling that Los Altos should remain our home. After leading the Adult Bible Fellowship (a class I would later come to see as a church in its own right) for about two years and seeing the Lord bless us with people coming to faith and being discipled, I was invited to join the staff of the church. My focus was to do the best job I could at shepherding people and making disciples, and I set out to do this with the tools and insights I had at the time.

Soon after I joined the staff, Dave Marksbury, an elder in our church and our denomination's director of church planting for the West Coast, invited me to be a part of a newly forming group that was to take responsibility for planting churches in southern California and Arizona. Neil Cole was also a part of this group that would one day become what is now known as CMA, Church Multiplication Associates. When we began CMA, we had a desire to plant traditional, denominational churches in our region. It seemed like a big goal to us, and we set out to make it happen.

It's hard for me to imagine what my life or the life of Los Altos Grace would be like had I not accepted that invitation to get involved in planting churches. This is really where my journey toward organic church life began. It's hard for me to separate my personal journey from the journeys of CMA and Los Altos Grace. We have been intertwined now for more than two decades. I believe that God has used this intriguing pairing of interests and responsibilities to open the eyes of many to the organic principles of church life.

In the early days of CMA, we planted a number of traditional churches. Some were more successful than others, and some were outright failures. It's the failures that really caught our attention. We discovered, through trial and error, that even if you have lots of money, wonderful leaders, and a great strategy that's implemented with precision, you can fail. The most notable example was a church plant in northern San Diego County. We invested $100,000 in its first year, sent two pastors, blitzed the neighborhood with an advertising campaign, and opened the church with an attendance over three hundred. Great job! Within a year the church was closed. This catastrophic failure forced us to ask God what we were doing wrong.

We began earnestly seeking the Lord's direction. We were soon convinced that our biggest mistake was not doing so earlier. We were attempting to do God's work for Him. Instead of looking to Him for direction and seeking His power to accomplish His will, we wanted to create something we could give to Him as an offering. It may seem subtle, but we were offering Him the work of our hands. We found that this is not something that Almighty God is all that interested in.

About this time, I read a book by Larry Richards called *Church Leadership*.[1] The main thing I took away from it was the idea that Jesus is the Head of His body and that the body must be surrendered to Him if it is to be healthy and useful in accomplishing His purposes in this world. After reading the book (a couple of times, mind you), I was so excited about my new discoveries that I decided to share them with the elders of Los Altos Grace.

By this time I had been called as senior pastor. I planned a retreat, packaged a curriculum designed to enlighten all who would attend, and spent an entire weekend immersing the elders in it. It was an intense time of theological discussion and debate. We were trying to understand the nature and purpose of the church. Is it an organization or an organism? Is it to be led by men or by God? What role does the Holy Spirit play in guiding, directing, and empowering each and every believer, and what can church leaders do or not do to encourage this process? I was proposing that church should be less like a business and more like a family. I also argued that we should be less interested in programming desired to attract people and get them involved in church-prescribed ministries and more interested in helping them hear directly from Jesus and personally follow His leading. At the end of our time together, the first comment I received was "I wouldn't want to go to a church like that!" And the second was like it: "If we leave everything up to the Holy Spirit, nothing will ever get done." Ouch! I could see we were in for a long haul.

This experience taught me that a work of God in the hearts and minds of His children is necessary if their eyes are to be opened and their minds are to be changed. I was wrong to dump everything I'd learned on them in a weekend and expect that it would bring dynamic change. Instead, I discovered that what's needed is patience, prayer, and agonizing discussion. God changes people at different times and at different rates. I found that I couldn't treat this like some new program I wanted to institute. Taking time to learn from God together made all the difference.

Over the next couple of years, the elders, staff, and I had many discussions, searched the Scriptures together, and prayed about these issues. Some of those elders never did see the value in this not-so-new approach. These men of God chose to leave our fellowship rather than stand in the way. It's always hard to separate from people, but we've done so in love and have been for the most part able to maintain good relationships with each other.

Today, the leaders of Los Altos Grace are fully vested in living out patterns of life that produce more life. This is how we understand the term *organic*. It's about seeing that the life of Jesus is permeating the lives of His disciples and that they are seeing that life reproduced in others. These changes in mind-set have had a profound effect on the way we conduct ourselves as a church.

We no longer see leadership as an office to hold or a task to accomplish; we see it as a calling of God. The responsibility of leadership is to encourage life and health in the body and help its members become fully functioning disciples of Jesus who have each been called for a particular purpose. We focus much less on creating events to attract outsiders and instead encourage each believer to reach out to others whom God puts in their path or to look for pockets of people who need Jesus and bring the light to them.

To the untrained eye, Los Altos continues to look like an average traditional church. We have a preschool and an elementary school. We meet on Sundays for worship and a sermon and offer Sunday school to children and adults. We run a weeklong camp for kids every summer and have groups for youth, college students, men, and women. Sounds pretty normal, doesn't it?

But if you look more closely, there are differences. The people of this church are a family. Each group, from the Sunday school classes to the men's and women's groups, constitutes a spiritual family. Group members share life together, care for one another's needs, and build one another up in the faith. The overall community of Los Altos is complex. Many people belong to more than one spiritual family and move easily from one group to another and back again. There is an ethos of connectedness. We rejoice with each other and grieve with each other. There is a profound knowledge of the Lord and His Word. It is part of our culture to want to understand the truth and live by it. It is also part of our culture to seek the presence, power, and guidance of God for every situation, whether personal or corporate. We believe that

God desires to use every disciple to bring His goodness to a world that badly needs it. As a result, we spend more time and effort helping people discover their own unique callings and spheres of influence than we do trying to orchestrate opportunities of service for them.

The kids' camp that we run every year has become a leadership farm system of sorts. Elementary-age children who attend the camp have lots of fun and learn much about the Lord. As they enter middle school, they become counselor assistants and activity support staff and then later move on to work as counselors and leaders. The result is that they grow up with a value for service to others, and this permeates their lifestyle as adults. A large majority of the church family participates in the camp and the opportunity to spend a week together, working hard and long, has a profound effect on the deepening of relationships across the age spectrum.

Our elder board has changed dramatically. We used to operate by Robert's Rules of Order and made decisions by majority rule. We still conduct business and make decisions, but now it's more like a brotherhood. We talk, we pray, and we talk some more. We wait until we have a unanimous sense that God is moving. We haven't taken a vote in years. Sometimes this is difficult. Things can move slowly, and that can be frustrating. We have learned, though, to love and trust each other and to respect the Spirit of God that is present in each of us. Over and over again, the Lord has demonstrated that if we wait for Him, we will not be disappointed.

Our focus in meetings is more about the health and well-being of the church family than it is about the machinations of the organization. We spend a lot of time praying for various needs within the body and for spiritual growth and awareness for individuals and the whole group. We consistently resist the temptation to put much energy into planning events or organizing ministry opportunities. Instead, we have purposely created a permission-giving environment so that individuals and groups feel free to make plans and get others involved as the Lord leads.

Let me share some examples of how this works. A college girl in our church family felt called to build a house for a poor family in Mexico. She had heard of an organization called Hands of

Mercy that helps churches do this sort of thing. In this case she approached a couple of the elders and asked what they thought. They encouraged her to share her idea with the church family at large and see if God generated any interest. She made an announcement, and people got very excited. As things started to get organized, she soon found that the level of interest in her project was higher than expected. She enlisted the help of other college students and some adults in making and carrying out their plans. When all was said and done, the church family had given more than $15,000 for the construction of three small homes. More than two hundred people of all ages participated in building the components of the homes, and more than eighty traveled with the houses to Mexico and helped assemble them.

Many churches do projects similar to this one. What was different about this experience is that this project was not even on the radar for the church leaders. When they were approached, they didn't think about whom to ask but instead immediately encouraged this young woman to pursue the task that God had given her. The result was a wonderful opportunity for the church family to work together for the good of the less fortunate and a boost in the faith and confidence of a young woman who desires to be used of God.

It doesn't always go this smoothly. Sometimes people wish to do things that seem to be at odds with the direction in which the church is moving. Let me share another example involving college students.

A group of talented young men desired to start a Sunday evening service for college students. They believed they could establish an event that would attract others their age and give them an opportunity to make disciples. When I first heard of their plan, I was not enthused. As a church, we had been moving away from initiating any new attractional ministries. After extensive discussions with the young men, it became clear that they believed God had called them to start this new ministry. Because I want to promote the value of a life lived in response to the leading of God, I felt it necessary to encourage these young men in their venture. For me, it wasn't about whether or not they would be successful but rather whether or not there were lessons for them to learn by stepping out on faith in God.

They started their service and focused on creating a comfortable environment for worship and learning. They took full responsibility for planning and leading this weekly event. They attracted a small but consistent group who learned a great deal about truth and how to defend it. The group met regularly for about a year and then less regularly as the young leaders' lives became complicated with things such as marriage, work, and school. All in all it was a great exercise, and people were touched in the process.

What I want you to understand here is that this is not something I or the elders would have considered doing, yet in the final analysis, we had no problem encouraging these young men to follow their passion and sense of calling. Had we stopped them by saying no, we would have succeeded only at limiting their development as true followers of Jesus.

We place a high value on listening to and following Christ. We want all the members of our spiritual family to know that they are useful to God and act on that knowledge. As the years have passed, the culture of our church has become more and more accepting of these truths, and the result is that I regularly find out about new house churches, Bible studies, and service ministries after they have started or even sometimes after they've been completed.

Mike Jentes, a coworker in the faith and fellow shepherd of our spiritual family, has called Los Altos a church with a traditional skin and an organic soul. I couldn't agree more. We are fully aware that God is still at work conforming us to His image, and this is the reality that keeps us going. There is still much that He desires to accomplish in our midst.

Some transfusional observations: Unlike the first two examples, the transfusion of Los Altos was not initiated in response to some precipitating event or condition. And unlike the first two examples, Los Altos was not led to divest itself of its property. But like the first two, the changes began with a change in the pastor's own understanding. The changes in this situation were more slowly implemented and less perceptible to people on the outside, but the same processes of fostering and submitting to new insights was at work.

Los Altos moved from trying to attract outsiders to enabling members to follow Christ, with the result that those members consistently bring Christ to outsiders. The church moved from thinking of itself as an organization to seeing itself as a family of families. The leaders had enough conviction in the organic reality of the body of Christ that they were willing to pay a price for it, and they did. The fruit of the ministry is born naturally from the people instead of initiated from the top down, even when that ministry may not be among the top desires of the leadership.

VALLEYLIFE GRACE, PHOENIX VALLEY, ARIZONA

ValleyLife Grace was started using a cell church model. Ed Waken, founding pastor, church planter, and now an integral part of the CMA team, set out with a goal to build a church thirty thousand strong. He'd be the first to tell you that much of that goal had to do with wanting to make a name for himself and secure a place of significance in history. Like many pastors, Ed drew his sense of self-worth and significance from his ability to perform and accomplish what he believed was the mission God had given him. Today, even if you looked really hard, you'd be hard pressed to find that Ed.

As is true in most cases, the transformation of ValleyLife began with the transformation of its pastor. Once the church began, the cell structure tended to drive the flow of ministry, and the push to grow drove people to perform. Though the church began in homes, there was soon a desire for a corporate meeting. This was in some part due to old ways of thinking and in some part due to the need for money to support the church and its pastor.

Once the church reached about a hundred people, the growth seemed to stop. They had reached a plateau, and even though they tried such things as better music, better locations, shorter sermons, and fun activities, nothing enabled them to push through the wall they hit.

It was at this point that Ed began to discover organic principles along with CMA. Ed began to see that his pride and need to feel significant were obstacles to what God wanted to accomplish. He repented of these things and started looking for new ways to help others grow and serve. After reading *Church Leadership* by

Larry Richards and concluding that Christ needed to be free to lead His church, Ed met with the leaders and began to talk with them about the things he was learning. Ed says he had to step down from being the go-to guy and the answer man. He had to learn to value the input of others and often choose their way over his. He realized that this was an acknowledgment that the voice of God could come through any believer and that he, as the pastor, was not Christ's sole channel. As Ed changed and positioned himself in a different place as a leader, the church changed too.

ValleyLife is now a network of autonomous churches ranging in size from ten to twenty members. Each home church makes its own decisions and follows the path God sets out for it. Sometimes this means walking together in relationship with other groups or the whole, and other times it means striking out independently. Either way, Christ is given the lead. The DNA (detailed in Chapters Two and Three) and Life Transformation Groups (LTGs)[2] became integral parts of the community of ValleyLife. The DNA is the vision for each disciple and group, and the entire church is evaluated by it. The expectation is that if the DNA is present and active, the disciple and the church will be healthy and reproductive. Life Transformation Groups are the backbone of how disciples are made and infused with the DNA.

Ed says it took time to reeducate the leaders and the church about the DNA and the need to listen to God and be led by the Spirit. These teachings were at first met with resistance and at times even anger. As Ed resisted the temptation to be the go-to guy and pushed people toward Jesus for answers to their questions and problems, they hated it at first. But as they became more comfortable in their own relationships with Christ, that anger and resistance turned to freedom and joy.

Not everyone has welcomed the changes. ValleyLife has experienced conflict from both sides of the spectrum. Many who come to check out the church are just looking for a new way to have their needs met. They are often unwilling to embrace the DNA and let it permeate and transform their lives. When these people are met with the consistent unwillingness of others to take responsibility for their life and growth, they become disenchanted and often leave in a huff. On the other hand, some have taken organic principles to extremes and used their particular hobbyhorse to try to rein in and control others. This inflexibility recently resulted in a church split. From Ed's perspective, this resulted in one more organic network serving the Phoenix valley.

Today, ValleyLife still has a weekly corporate gathering, but there is no pressure for everyone to be involved. The gatherings have taken on a new flavor. People are free to interact, ask questions, offer input, and even give direction. The focus is no longer on worship and a sermon, and the time together can take many forms. It can be a time of equipping and training or a time of community service, testimony, or prayer. The Spirit dictates, and the people follow.

Besides meeting with their respective churches, the leaders of each church now meet weekly. They don't do this because there is so much more to be done but because they enjoy being together and praying for God's direction for people and the spiritual health of the church. They no longer move forward with decisions affecting the body unless they are in full agreement. They recognize that God is doing something special, want to stay in step with Him, and are excited to be a part of it.

ValleyLife's vision is simple: make disciples of Jesus who will make disciples of Jesus.

Some transfusional observations: ValleyLife started as a cell church, so from a structural perspective, it was closer to what people imagine an organic church to be. It's important to see that even though the church was operating with a more decentralized model, significant change was still necessary. Being a new church plant, ValleyLife was also able to experience a more rapid change with less upheaval than the previous examples, but it nevertheless had to pay a price—and is still doing so.

God had to make changes in the way Ed thought of himself and the church. As Ed submitted himself to these changes, God began to change ValleyLife. As with all the examples we've shared, these changes were initially met with resistance, but over time the new ways of thinking and living became normative. The role of leadership shifted dramatically from being authoritative and directive to freely distributing authority to others. As members have accepted responsibility for their own individual walk with Christ, the church family as a whole has been infused with new life and energy. DNA became the core of the church by reproducing healthy disciples who carry the DNA within them.

NEW SONG, IRVINE, CALIFORNIA

Dave Gibbons began New Song Church in Irvine, California, and built it with great skill into what is probably the largest Asian American church in the United States. Dave is a strong leader and did everything a successful senior pastor would do for fast growth.

After about a decade of leading this church, Dave took a one-year sabbatical and moved his family to Bangkok, Thailand. His intent was to start a new church there as he had done in Irvine. But he found that what works in Orange County, California, doesn't necessarily work in Thailand.

Through trial and error and doing what any good missionary should do—listening to the indigenous people—he discovered that a more organic approach was better. New Song Bangkok was started. This church was centered around life together. When people met, they sat in circles instead of the typical theater-style seating. Dave's house became "church" as people came through his condo doors 24/7. His doors remained unlocked. It wasn't church as a program but church as family. The emphasis was on rich relationships, loving others without strings.

Dave returned to the mother church in California with a new vision for what could be done. He announced that New Song in Irvine would become more organic. Few congregants really knew what this entailed, but they soon found out.

With this organic concept of church in Dave's heart, the leaders looked at themselves with new lenses that helped them find a unique purpose for their mission to the world and the kingdom. For instance, being mostly an Asian American church, they understood what being "third culture" is all about. When someone is not from a single culture but because they have grown up under the influence of two cultures, they actually are in a real sense a third culture, made up of influences of both. Those who are third-culture have the ability to adapt to multiple cultures.

A holy sense of calling is evident within this church, as its members see themselves as uniquely designed by God to be entrepreneurial and at home in a rapidly changing world. Suddenly, they were not just trying to live out the ministry vision of other megaministries as they once had. Being born in an Asian American context, New Song had a sense of identity, which became a strong platform from which to launch kingdom enterprise into the world that the previous models that they may have followed could never do. They were not just trying to adapt someone else's ministry ideas; they were free to create whole new ideas never attempted before.

One of the first things they did was change the way they used staff. They would no longer be specialists that do the ministry but would instead be generalists who equip others to do the ministry. Rather than just executing programs, their main role became highly developing others. This alone is a radical shift in how the average church functions. Some of the staff who were originally hired to do what they loved to do found that they needed to find somewhere else to go. As certain popular staff members left, parishioners who were drawn to these leaders were also inclined to leave. The church lost numbers of people and the offerings that those people brought in. Nevertheless, church leaders pursued this new God-led direction. They experienced nearly a 40 percent decline in the church! Dave felt God saying, "Develop three hundred radicals." He didn't know God was getting truly literal with him. In the midst of declining numbers and diminishing confidence, they continued to pursue this new God-led direction.

The leadership of New Song has learned that its greatest asset is not in its staff, a weekly worship service, or facilities but in the people that make up the church. The leaders decided to release these people and to network them so as to create new ideas that benefit not just the weekly meetings of the church but also the kingdom of God in general and even the world at large. This shift in values and resulting focus has given birth to a myriad of fresh enterprises that are helping reshape culture and the future. It is not only the releasing of talented and creative people that has increased their influence but also the synergy found in networking and blending these diverse creative skill sets and domains of influence.

With old boundaries such as worship attendance and a geographical address no longer a hindrance to New Song's members, they found that their influence was spreading all over the place. Today you can find churches in Los Angeles, New York, Bangkok,

Mexico City, Brazil, London, India, and Japan. You will also find influence in the arts, technology, business, the nonprofit world, education, publishing, and even church ministry. Their formation of a human development organization called XEALOT is a great example of this type of synergistic work. XEALOT is an expression of a global platform that customizes the development of artists, business leaders, and community development workers. They may have lost some numbers of people in the beginning of their transfusional process, but they have gained tenfold in numbers of people influenced and influencing since that time. Today the church is rocking with third-culture people and constantly growing in its diversity. It sees itself as a launching pad to the world. New Song's metrics are no longer about Sunday morning numbers but instead about the number of Monday morning radicals living life fully equipped to make a difference in their domain of influence.[3]

Some transfusional observations: First, the change begins with the heart of the leader; as you have seen, this is a consistent ingredient in any transfusion. Second, that the DNA found in the disciple is the greatest resource in the church, and influence develops from there rather than from a boardroom or the desk of a single leader. Third, the leadership of the church had to shift from being specialists that did the ministry work to people who equipped others for the work of ministry. Fourth, New Song counted the cost and paid a price for the change. Fifth, the church is an example to us all of not only releasing ordinary Christ followers to make an impact on their world but also actively equipping them to do so. Sixth, New Song began to reproduce naturally via empowerment of people who have natural relationships in other locales. Finally, New Song found the various contexts of society where their disciples were found to be the ideal place for their ministry to flourish.

COMPARING AND CONTRASTING THE TRANSFUSED CHURCHES

These churches are all very different and were chosen partly for that very reason. We do not want you to blindly follow their example but rather to learn from them all and discover what your own unique process of transfusion will be like. Two of these churches were many decades old before transfusion occurred, and three were very young church plants. The Well was Southern Baptist, Los Altos and ValleyLife were Grace Brethren, Vineyard Central was a Vineyard church, and New Song was Evangelical Covenant. It is also significant that the transfused churches do not appear to be stuck in their denominational model or mind-set, and many of them are becoming agents of change within their denominations.

All of them began with leadership willing to lead them through change whatever the cost. Each began to value relationships over programs and empowered ordinary Christ followers to expand the kingdom of God in the marketplace. All of them reproduced disciples before reproducing groups of believers. In each example, the leadership shifted to equipping others to do the ministry and stopped carrying the ministry load for the church. These churches have also come to see that the true place of ministry is in the places where people live, work, and play and that it's not just confined to a church campus.

We do not hold these churches up as perfect examples and do not promise that they will always remain healthy, strong, and vibrant. What we will commit to is that in their story so far they have been courageous and willing to sacrifice everything in the pursuit of Christ, and lives have been changed permanently and positively because of that.

Transforming a highly structured and controlled organization into a freely reproducing movement takes a miracle, the miracle of resurrection. As Christians, we of all people should be believers in resurrection, but in order to experience a resurrection, something else is needed first, and that is what Chapter Five is about.

This concludes Part One of the book. In this part we have done our best to demonstrate that change is necessary and only possible with God. Part Two lays out many of the practical implications of seeing a church transfused with the life of Christ and changed from the inside out.

PART TWO

IMPLEMENTING CHANGE FROM THE INSIDE OUT

CHAPTER FIVE

DYING AS IF YOUR LIFE DEPENDED ON IT

In every city in America there is at least one church with a building worth hundreds of thousands (if not millions) of dollars. This church meets every Sunday morning with only eight to ten silver- and blue-haired women and one or two balding gentlemen for a "service." They sing a hymn or two, one of the gentlemen shares a few opinions of things in the world today, they say a prayer, murmur amen, and then go home.

Empty parking spaces, silent pulpits, and dusty pews cry out for days of glory gone by. The church has been dead for years, perhaps decades, but has been kept alive by an artificial life support system. The soul is gone, brain waves have ceased, but mechanization keeps the lungs breathing, the heart beating, and the door opening every Sunday morning at precisely 10:00 a.m.

Why? We are so desperately afraid to admit failure that we will keep the church as we know it alive as long as we can. It is as if the continuity of Christianity depends on this one church staying alive. If the church dies, God has failed, and we cannot allow that.

Why are we so desperate to keep churches alive? Although we know that the church is special to Jesus (His bride!), we think we have lost touch with something very spiritual: death. Can it be that death is as spiritually right as life?

THE SIN OF SELF-PRESERVATION

While we clearly avoid a theology of death, the opposite is not a theology of life, for life is not what you will find in churches that strive to avoid death at all costs. I (Neil) don't know how it happened, but at some point in history we bought into a theology of *safety*. We think that we should do what is safe—for ourselves, for our families, and for our churches. In fact, we are convinced that anything that is unsafe must be outside of God's will and is thoroughly un-American and un-Christian. A theology of safety is put in place as a defensive measure to avoid death. This leads us right down the path of self-preservation at all costs.

Jesus is not about safety. He is the one who said things like "I send you out as sheep in the midst of wolves" (Matt. 10:16), "I did not come to bring peace, but a sword" (Matt. 10:34) "He who loves son or daughter more than Me is not worthy of Me." (Matt. 10:37), and "Let the dead bury the dead—you follow Me" (Matt. 8:22). These are not safe and wholesome, family-friendly words; they are words that shake us up and toss us out in the deep end far beyond what is safe.

We often approach church and ministry with a theology focused on what is SAFE:

Self-preservation = our mission
Avoidance of the world and risk = wisdom
Financial security = responsible faith
Education = maturity

Does that not describe many of the churches or ministries you have encountered? Some of you have been on elder or deacon boards that are perfectly described by this acronym. I know I have. In fact, it almost seems like our default response. Our instinct is to do whatever it takes to preserve our life. It is a fight to stay close to a theology of death.

Preserving oneself separate from God's life is not just a sin; it is blasphemy. It is taking your own place as the life-giver. Self-preservation means that you are the one who gives and sustains life, which is blasphemous. It is also the path to self-destruction, not life. As Jesus said so strongly and repeatedly, "The one who finds his life loses it" (Matt. 10:39). As a consequence of the sin of self-preservation, literally hundreds of thousands of Christians and churches are deceived into a "Churchianity" that is carried out by men, for men, under the name of God.

Johannes Hoekendijk, a Dutch theologian who taught at Union Theological Seminary in New York during the 1950s, had a great impact on expanding the mission of the ecumenical church movement beyond merely extending the church-ruled culture of Christendom. He believed that the *missio dei* was larger than establishing larger church boundaries. He is said to have defined the church's well-being as "when she cannot count on anything anymore but God's promises." That is life! And that is what faith is meant to look like.

Self-preservation is actively choosing an alternative to the life of our God. It is a direct move away from faith in the life-giving and life-sustaining Savior. God created us with an instinct for self-preservation. It is not a sin to want to live. It is human instinct to want to survive. It is a sin, however, to choose to live without God as our life source. We can use that desire to live as motivation to die, for that is the only path that leads to true life in God's upside-down kingdom.

When presented with the choice of self-preservation or the cross, the choice for the servant of God should be clear. We follow Christ to the cross or we do not follow Him at all. He said, "If anyone wishes to come after Me, let him deny himself, pick up his cross daily, and follow Me" (Luke 9:23–25).

Just as Jesus picked up our cross and died in our place, we need to pick up His and die for Him. Dying to oneself is not easy at all and runs contrary to one's own instinctive response, but it is right nonetheless. Choosing not to go the path of death and instead to choose to preserve your own life is actually to choose death. This fear that we have of suffering loss or harm is a primary tool of the enemy. He uses it to paralyze us and keep us from being effective as the people of God. As the writer to the Hebrews notes, "Since the children share in flesh and blood, He Himself likewise also partook of the same, that through death He might render powerless him who had the power of death, that is, the devil, and might free those who through fear of death were subject to slavery all their lives" (Heb. 2:14–15).

As we have explained in Chapter One, the kingdom of God is upside down and counterintuitive. Life comes from death; you can't get more of a paradox than that.

Carrying Your Cross

Death is more then just an important idea for discipleship—it is absolutely essential. Without a death, there is no disciple. Without a dying to self, we do not have life within us.

Jesus said clearly, "He who does not take up his cross and follow Me is not worthy of Me" (Matt. 10:39a). We tend to think of the cross with the baggage of two thousand years of religious worship and celebration, removed from the New Testament. It is a sacred symbol to us. We wear gold crosses around our necks. The image adorns our buildings and probably hangs somewhere in your home. The symbol has come to represent Christianity, and in some respects rightfully so. The cross is the hinge of all history. It is the centerpiece of all we believe and hold dear.

We have heard sermons of how the burdens of life are "our cross to bear." We must jettison all that and look at the statement for what it meant, literally, to those who heard the words for the first time. They knew what it meant to see a man carrying a cross. They had seen the horrific act many times. It meant only one thing, and suffering the struggles of life were hardly it. Carrying a cross was a death sentence fulfilled. The man who carried the cross had no way out. His life was over, and he was about to suffer the most humiliating and painful execution ever devised. He was a dead man walking.

The disciples may not have understood that Jesus Himself was about to carry a cross to His own vicious execution, but they knew well what Jesus was talking about. Wearing a cross around your neck is like wearing a guillotine around your neck or an electric chair, only worse.

The cross was an instrument of capital punishment more severe than any other. It was so severe that simply being a Roman citizen excluded you from ever having to suffer such a fate no matter what crime you committed. Carrying the cross was a death sentence, and the disciples understood it as such. Ironically, we are the ones, with a clear view of history and centuries of learning, who do not.

We are unworthy of Jesus when we resist our own death to self. He was willing to give His life for us, and unless we are willing to return the favor, we do not deserve to wear the mantle of His sacrifice. The odd thing is that it's our view of life that is twisted. The Bible makes it clear that the one who has faith in Jesus has already passed from death to life and from darkness to light. The writer to the Hebrews put it this way: "'I will never leave you or forsake you.' So that we may say with confidence, 'The Lord is my helper. What can man do to me?'" (Heb. 13:6). Physical death is nothing to God. We should learn to see it for what it really is.

EMBRACING A THEOLOGY OF DEATH

Jesus went on to say, "He who has found his life will lose it, and he who has lost his life for My sake will find it" (Matt. 10:39b).

Why is death to self so important? Consider this: without death, you cannot have a resurrection. Without death, there would not be any gospel or salvation or even life itself. Perhaps it is time that we embrace a theology of death.

This is what a theology of death looks like:

Die daily to who we are and what we want.
Empowering others, not self, is our life.
Accept risk as normative.
Theology is not just knowledge but practice.
Hold tight to Christ and loosely to everything else.

Unless we are willing to die, we will not live. It is that simple. Death is the path to life. Conversely, holding on to life appears to be the path to death. We are to die to self because it is the only way we can live for Jesus. We can only have one master. Either we will live for ourselves or we will live for Jesus. This is why we must put ourselves to death every day.

Our cultural mind-set in the West places the individual first and foremost. We read verses that use the second person plural and apply them to ourselves as individuals when in fact they are addressed to a community as a whole rather than to us alone.

There are many cultures, however, that do not see the world that way. They immediately regard life as a community first and an individual second.

The words of Jesus having to do with death are most commonly applied to the individual disciple. And granted, the verse should be applied in this way. We have found, though, that the truth in His words is universal and applies to any organization made up of disciples, such as a church.

D Is for Dying

More than once, in fact, I (Neil) have found myself being the voice of doom to a dying organization or ministry. I have "pulled the plug" on more than a few ministries, from a Bible study to a Sunday school class to a church and even a denominational publishing ministry.

What is ironic is that all the different ministries that I have had the courage to lead toward death *have never died.* If anything, they were already dead; I simply said it out loud. There is a sense of freedom that comes when someone has the courage to say what everyone else is already thinking but terrified to say out loud. When we actually pulled the plug publicly, the ministries were all reborn with new life and new vision—better, even, than they had ever been. That is when I discovered that these truths that Jesus has given us are to be applied corporately as well as individually.

When we fear death, we have lost sight of the gospel. Perhaps that is why we are so ineffective in preaching the gospel: we don't really believe it! If we did believe it, we would accept the words: "Death is swallowed up in victory. O death, where is your victory? O death, where is your sting?" (1 Cor. 15:54–55).

In fact, we have come to believe that the health of any organization can be evaluated in direct proportion to its willingness to die. The more vested it is in self-preservation, the less healthy it will be. The more willing to die so that the kingdom can flourish, the healthier the organization. Where does your church ministry stand in this regard?

There are important implications for Christian leadership in this discussion of death and resurrection. As leaders, it is important that we lead by going first. You cannot lead where you do not go. We must all go to the cross; that is where leadership begins.

Once you have been crucified, you are a different person. Old things have "passed away," and "new things have come" (2 Cor. 5:17). A dead leader is a dangerous leader. Such a person has nothing left to lose. No personal glory is at stake. No rewards. Ambition is dead. There is no agenda but what is asked of the leader by Jesus. A dead person has no possessions to protect. You can't even really tempt a dead person; corpses feel no pain and have no lust. Dead people do not get their feelings hurt or feel offended by what has been said or not said. Once we pass through death, what else is there to fear?

When you have died with Christ, you see people differently. You are no longer looking out for your own personal interests because you don't have any, so now you can much more easily be concerned for others. Your decisions are no longer about what is best for yourself but what is best for the other person. This is where an empowerment strategy begins for the leader in the church.

A church that has died to what it has been or what it hopes it will become is a church that can become all that Christ desires it to be. As long as a church clings to past success or failures, it will be stuck in the past and will have little influence in the present or the future. A church that remains stuck in the attempt to fulfill some vision that never really came from God will likely never fulfill its own vision or the better one God has for it.

E Is for Empowerment

Jesus did not come to gain permission and empowerment but to give it away. He said, "The Son of man did not come to be served but to serve and to give His life a ransom for many" (Mark 10:45). Those who would follow Christ must follow His example.

Empowerment is not just for leaders; it is also for congregations. Imagine what would happen if the Brethren church in your town were more concerned with the success of the Baptist church. What would happen to the spiritual climate of a city if the local Presbyterian church were praying for the success of the

Pentecostal church and vice versa? I cannot help but believe that if the churches that make up the body of Christ, the one body of Christ, were to empower and lift up one another rather than attempt to ride each other's failure into their own success, a whole town or city would be transformed. The gospel would not just be preached but demonstrated in power. This can happen when a congregation is willing to take up its cross and die. Perhaps your church should lead the way.

A Is for Accepting Risk

Someone has said, "Faith is spelled R-I-S-K." We cannot truly have faith that is safe; we must be willing to embrace risk to live by faith, both individually and corporately. Faith in many churches has become nothing more than a piece of paper with a few doctrinal statements written out and agreed to by the people as a sort of pledge in order to be welcomed as a member. But faith is so much more than this. In many churches, faith is equated with "being faithful," demonstrated through regular attendance, being dependable, and handling your responsibilities with quiet reserve. These are all noble qualities, but faith is so much more than that!

We recommend that your leadership team wrestle with the following questions: What would it look like for our church if we were to take a big risk in faith so that it is only Jesus that will keep us alive? What would we attempt if we knew we could not fail? Now ask, even if we thought we would fail, is there something so valuable that it is still worth trying anyway? What would we be willing to risk in order to become more like Jesus than we are today? How far will we go when it comes to risking safety for Jesus' sake? Are we willing to risk death as an organization in the service of Christ?

T Is for Theology Lived Out in Practice

Doctrine is not a set of beliefs but a way of living. D. L. Moody is credited as saying, "The Scriptures were not given to increase our knowledge but to change our lives." In Titus 2 Paul espouses what sound doctrine is, and it is not Calvinism, Arminianism, Dispensationalism, or Pentecostalism. It says nothing of a Millennial

Kingdom or a Hypostatic Union. Sound doctrine according to Titus 2 is as follows:

> Older men are to be temperate, dignified, sensible, sound in faith, in love, in perseverance. Older women likewise are to be reverent in their behavior, not malicious gossips nor enslaved to much wine, teaching what is good, so that they may encourage the young women to love their husbands, to love their children, to be sensible, pure, workers at home, kind, being subject to their own husbands, so that the word of God will not be dishonored. Likewise urge the young men to be sensible; in all things show yourself to be an example of good deeds, with purity in doctrine, dignified, sound in speech which is beyond reproach, so that the opponent will be put to shame, having nothing bad to say about us. Urge bondslaves to be subject to their own masters in everything, to be well-pleasing, not argumentative, not pilfering, but showing all good faith so that they will adorn the doctrine of God our Savior in every respect. For the grace of God has appeared, bringing salvation to all men, instructing us to deny ungodliness and worldly desires and to live sensibly, righteously and godly in the present age, looking for the blessed hope and the appearing of the glory of our great God and Savior, Christ Jesus, who gave Himself for us to redeem us from every lawless deed, and to purify for Himself a people for His own possession, zealous for good deeds. [Titus 2: 2–14]

James is clear as well when he says emphatically:

> What use is it, my brethren, if someone says he has faith but he has no works? Can that faith save him? If a brother or sister is without clothing and in need of daily food, and one of you says to them, "Go in peace, be warmed and be filled," and yet you do not give them what is necessary for their body, what use is that? Even so faith, if it has no works, is dead, being by itself.
> But someone may well say, "You have faith and I have works; show me your faith without the works, and I will show you my faith by my works." You believe that God is one. You do well; the demons also believe, and shudder. But are you willing to recognize, you foolish fellow, that faith without works is useless? Was not Abraham our father justified by works when he offered up Isaac his son on the altar? You see that faith was working with his works, and as a result of the works, faith was perfected; and the Scripture

was fulfilled which says, "and Abraham believed God, and it was reckoned to him as righteousness," and he was called the friend of God. You see that a man is justified by works and not by faith alone. In the same way, was not Rahab the harlot also justified by works when she received the messengers and sent them out by another way? For just as the body without the spirit is dead, so also faith without works is dead. [James 2:14–26]

Just as a body without a spirit is a corpse, a church without faith that translates into action is a dead church. As we have said before, the church of the West is educated beyond its obedience, and more education is not the solution. We need more obedience. Another sermon will never be enough.

Frankly, pastor, we place way too much value on sermonizing. Another sermon is not going to change the world, the church, or even the person preaching. It is not the content of the sermon but obedience to God's Word that changes lives. I (Neil) remember once sitting alone working on the final touches of what was going to be a masterpiece sermon and hearing God's voice whisper in my ear, "Neil, Neil, (sigh) you know, you are never going to preach a sermon that ignites the third Great Awakening." I realized at that moment that I was not sent to preach sermons but the gospel—and there is a difference. I was called to make disciples who obey all that Jesus commanded, not parishioners who know a lot about the Bible. That was a life-changing moment for me. From that moment on, I invested my life in multiplying Christ followers. Frankly, I think my preaching got better for it, not worse.

Think about it: if your sermon was going to catalyze a revival, wouldn't it have happened by now? Pastors have been preaching every Sunday for hundreds of years; it is now time to obey all that Jesus commanded, not just talk about it.

H IS FOR HOLDING TIGHT TO CHRIST BUT RELEASING YOUR GRASP ON ALL ELSE

So much greed, selfishness, and stinginess in the kingdom of God is excused under the banner of "good stewardship." We believe that the tighter you hold on to Christ, the looser your grip on other things will be. There is an absolute and direct corollary between these two opposites. The harder you cling to things, the less you are holding on to Christ. If you find that as a church you have a difficult time giving away the use of facilities or equipment, perhaps that means you are not holding on to Christ with enough faith.

We know of a senior pastor of a church in our area who, after refurbishing the facilities with fresh paint and new carpet, stood before the congregation with a cup of coffee. To the shock and sighs of the congregation, he then intentionally poured its contents directly onto the new carpet, creating a dark puddle and a permanent stain. He said to the church that the carpet can go to hell but he didn't want the kids in the neighborhood to have to. The people outside the walls are far more important than the carpet inside of them. They left the stain as a permanent reminder that the mission is not in the building, but outside in the streets. We must not let our grasp of material things keep us from the mission we are actually called to and then excuse it under the banner of being good stewards.

We believe with all our hearts that a church that is overtly generous with all the resources it has been blessed with will always have enough to do whatever God has called it to. We also believe that greater resources come to the churches that are generous. A generous church is one that Jesus will want to increase and multiply. A greedy church is one that He will not want more of.

We would all agree that Jesus was a faithful steward, right? Well, I think we should take a second look at his financial practices. He had a band of followers who were responsible men for the most part. He even had a professional bookkeeper-accountant who served as a tax collector on His team. When Christ chose someone to be responsible for the purse, He chose the only untrustworthy thief on the team. We do not believe that this was an accident or a blind spot on His part. The way Jesus views money and the way the church views money are two very different things.

Jesus never placed His faith in His financial balance; he placed it in His Father, and we should all do likewise. It is safe to assume that if God has blessed your congregation with some property, it is so that you can bless others, for that is His nature and way (Gen. 12: 1–3). It has been estimated that only 15 cents of every dollar received by a church is actually spent to benefit those outside its own membership.[1] Of course, that 15 cents includes money spent on all mission work that is to reach people who will hopefully become members of the church, so the percentage that is intentionally spent on people never expected to darken the door of the church is even less.

We find that churches that allow multiple congregations to use their facilities are not as clean or ordered—but are far more beautiful. Those that do so without charge are the most beautiful, and both of us have aspired to that kind of generosity in ministry.

The Cure for All That Ails Us

Death will cure every illness. In fact, poisoning and killing the body has sometimes been a way to find a cure for some diseases, as is the case with chemotherapy treatments for cancers. For the church, self-preservation leads to institutionalization, which we believe brings forth death. Once a church suffers from the hardening of the categories and establishes itself as an institution, it is on the path to dying.

Early on in our ministry, we decided that anything less than a multiplication movement would be a failure for us. With this goal in mind, we realized that one of the greatest threats to fostering a multiplication movement is institutionalization. In fact, when you really think about it, every denomination began as a church-planting movement. Somewhere along the way, these movements became sedentary and institutionalized; they lost the breath of life that propelled them initially and became all about self-preservation.

From the beginning, we wanted to prevent this from happening to us. At the very least, we wanted to delay the decay for as long as is possible. So we tackled the question even before the movement began: How do we keep our movement from being institutionalized? That was difficult to answer. We found that it cannot really be answered in a vacuum. While we were discussing it, we found ourselves asking, "What policy can we put in place now that will keep us from becoming institutionalized?" As the question came off our lips, we realized its irony. We were close to taking steps toward being institutionalized in our striving to not be. Instead, we simply prayed and asked God to give us the answer.

Once we were in the thick of the movement, faced with the decisions that come with growth and momentum, we learned what it takes not to fall victim to institutionalization. In answer to our prayers, Jesus' Word came back: "He who has found his life will lose it, and he who has lost his life for My sake will find it" (Matt. 10:39b). This is brilliant. It is the kingdom way. The way to stay alive in Jesus' upside-down kingdom is to die regularly. It also verifies what our experience revealed.

When we made decisions that obviously benefited our own existence, the Lord consistently disciplined us. Every decision designed to increase our security and income by maintaining exclusive rights to our material and implementing proprietary policies that were intending to increase the likelihood of our own preservation met with immediate negative consequences, and we all knew God was leading us to be more generous and less exclusive. The results of self-preservation are always death and dying. When we have made decisions that, for all intents and purposes, appear to be suicidal, God has always blessed us with life, resources, and fruitfulness.

Our small nonprofit organization, CMAResources, does not usually break even at the end of each year. God has kept us in business even while most Christian retail bookstores and even national chains such as Borders are closing down. We should not be continuing, and it is honestly not always a very sure thing that we will. Who knows—perhaps by the time you read this, we will have gone out of business. That is of course the risk and the price that we are willing to pay to be what God desires us to be. For many years we would host a large national gathering of organic church practitioners, and we lost thousands of dollars regularly. Why would we do this? We did so because we felt God telling us to do it. Our own sense of self-preservation would shout at us not to do it, but we listened to a different voice.

Our biggest source of income each year is from our Greenhouse training (it's not much income, so don't think we are getting rich on Greenhouses). We average more than one weekend Greenhouse training event every week somewhere in the world. To date, close to fifty thousand people have been trained to start churches organically by making disciples from lost and unconnected people. As the founders of Greenhouse, we are the sole source of the training, and that should present us with a unique opportunity for self-preservation via proprietary policies. Instead, we decided to give it all away. Early on, people asked us if they could have our PowerPoint presentations. When we faced this request, we decided that it was best to give it away free of charge but with a price of another sort. Our policy is to give it away without charge to anyone who has started three to five churches after taking the training. We do not want to contribute to the strange U.S. phenomenon of expert consultants who have never done the work, and for that reason we do ask that the people who receive our materials be proven practitioners. We grant permission to our trainers to conduct their own training, unconnected to our office, and to feel free to make the material their own. They can rename it, add to it, or even take some from it. They also have no obligation to send any financial support our way or share the revenue that such training can generate. All of these decisions are against the idea of self-preservation. This does not help the survivability of CMAResources, but it does contribute to the spread of the movement and does help increase our faith daily in God as our provider.

We can tell our own history by connecting suicidal organizational decisions together into a stream of strategically stupid choices that have brought incredible life and multiplication. Many of those choices had nothing to do with our own spiritual insight; we were just that stupid. Over time and with the rich experience of God's favor, though, we have begun to consciously choose death for CMA because it is the only way to stay alive and keep multiplying. We have learned through experience and the Father's loving discipline the value of living precariously rather than protectively according to the wisdom of the world. We have become more content existing in a place where God must intervene or all is lost. In fact, we are growing to like it. Like a long-distance runner who enjoys the endorphin rush, we live for the moments when God shows up with another miraculous provision in the heat of the battle just at the right moment.

It is fun to sit together and recount some of the ridiculous decisions we have made all along the way and how God has used these to show His provision of life, power, and resources. The foolish do confound the wise. The weak are strong. The last are first. The dead live. The kingdom is indeed upside down.

Not all of our foolish decisions were the right ones to make. Some of the things we've decided are frankly embarrassing. Nevertheless, finding ourselves on the verge of closing down as an organization, but for God's grace, is a dynamic and life-giving place to be. We have found that when you do not have much to protect, making risky decisions is far easier.

We suggest that you plan an all-day brainstorming session with key leaders around this subject: When was the last time we decided to do something that could hurt our organization but help others and chose to do it anyway? What would it look like for us to die in order to live? How would we communicate these ideas to the congregation? What would a preaching series on this look like, and how would we as an entire church die at the end of this series? What would a memorial service look like if we were to plan one? What would a wake look like for the church that dies? And what would a baby shower look like for what would be reborn? What can we decide to do in the next few weeks that will only benefit others and bring no benefit to ourselves?

The path to life begins at the gate called death. It is a narrow and dark gate that is foreboding and intimidating, but for those who know Christ, there is no fear and no pain in it, not even a sting.

Once you have died to yourself and are ready to initiate change empowered by new life, it is essential that you influence people in a new way. The old way creates a dependence on you, but the transfusional way empowers and releases people. Chapter Six addresses how we must detoxify from our dependence issues.

CHAPTER SIX

DETOXIFYING FROM DEPENDENCE

It is an unfortunate reality that people can become addicted to poisonous things. Chemical dependence is an ugly thing that wreaks havoc in our lives and in the lives of those we love. Drugs kill.

We have both watched many families destroyed by the powerful hold of chemical dependence. To break free, a person must go through a detoxification process that leads through withdrawal from the poison. Only then can the person rebuild his or her life and restore relationships to a healthy place. Even then, it is a fragile mend that can easily become unraveled if the addict takes up the chemical again. The temptation of the addiction seems to never really leave the addict's mind.

Codependence is when a loved one also finds his or her own sense of identity and purpose wrapped up in the ebb and flow of another person's dependence issues. If the husband is dependent on drugs and the wife is the codependent one, he behaves irresponsibly and leaves behind chaos and ruin while she runs around cleaning things up and making his addiction possible. She enables him in his dependence. This is a tragic and ruinous combination that we have seen time and time again.

We have dependence issues in the church, which are also leaving behind sick and weak churches. This dependence requires detoxification.

Like all families with dependence issues, we have an irresponsible party who is dependent on something and a codependent party that is enabling the problems. In our case, the common church attender is the irresponsible party who is dependent on the pastor's teaching to hear from God and feel good. These congregants have no desire to actually carry the responsibility of God's kingdom with them into their workplace or neighborhood. In fact, they are happy to let the clergy carry all the responsibility for them; after all, that's what clergy are paid to do.

Pastors are the codependent parties who enjoy feeling important and will gladly clean up the messes of their irresponsible attenders. They feel responsible, and their sense of identity is built around feeling important to the rest of the church. They value being needed and liked.

This is a dysfunctional situation that must be challenged and changed. The challenge should begin with ending the enabling. That is one important reason that this book is addressed to the leaders of the church. We firmly believe that if the people of God are to take responsibility for hearing directly from God and moving in obedience out into the world where they live and work, the leaders will have to stop enabling their lack of responsibility.

THE PROBLEM OF SELF-DECEPTION

A church built on this kind of mutual dependence cannot possibly be a true missional church; it can and will be only attractional. You can grow a church that has this sort of dependence, but you cannot multiply it. All the energy is flowing in one direction, toward the pastor; it is sucked into the center. A church established under this needy and codependent leadership can grow, but it will still be weak. We often refer to the "magnetic" personality of a pastor, and sadly, that is what some churches are built on. A magnetic personality will draw people toward it, but it will not send them forth. As we said earlier, you cannot suck water in and spit it out at the same time. As A. W. Tozer is said to have commented, "A church that can't worship must be entertained; and men who can't lead a church to worship must provide entertainment."

How many times have you heard a person evaluate a church based on the entertainment factor? So many times we've heard people tell us they chose a church based on the fact that they liked the music during worship. We've also heard people say that they left a church because they didn't like the music. We didn't know the worship was for you! Ultimately, this is the problem. A church established with a dependence on human beings is blasphemous, and worship becomes about self rather than God.

Every Sunday there are very expensive buildings full of people who arrive anticipating some nice program to inspire them for the week. Every Sunday across the country we have a small and exhausted group of leaders working hard to entertain the masses enough that they will be inspired to return the next week and hopefully drop some money in the offering basket so that the leaders can afford to put on a better show next week so as not to lose people to the other churches who are desperately trying to attract them too.

Perhaps the worst part of this scenario is the delusion. The pastor feels good about his or her popularity and thinks all must be well. The people also feel good with the "success" and the fact that their felt needs are being met, so they too believe this must be right. Both parties are happy with this scenario; therefore, it must be good, and God must be pleased. But nothing could be further from the truth.

It is possible as a church to think you are doing well when in fact you are very sick and near death. Of the seven letters to churches that Jesus sent in Revelation 2–3, almost half of the churches suffered from a form of self-deception, two in a negative way and a third in a positive manner.

To the church of Sardis, Jesus dictated to John the apostle, "I know your deeds, that you have a name that you are alive, but you are dead. Wake up, and strengthen the things that remain, which were about to die; for I have not found your deeds completed in the sight of My God."

To the church of Laodicea Jesus said, "Because you say, 'I am rich, and have become wealthy, and have need of nothing,' and you do not know that you are wretched and miserable and poor and blind and naked."

Even in a positive way a church can think it is worse off than it really is. To the church of Smyrna He wrote, "And to the angel of the church in Smyrna write: The first and the last, who was

Building a Church on Dependence

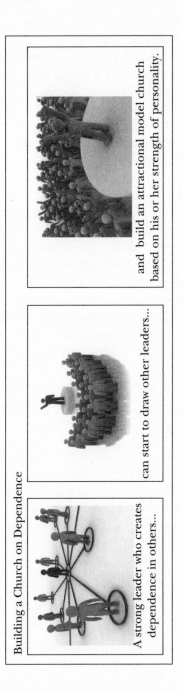

A strong leader who creates dependence in others...

can start to draw other leaders...

and build an attractional model church based on his or her strength of personality.

dead, and has come to life, says this: 'I know your tribulation and your poverty (but you are rich).'"

The worst part of self-deception is that by very definition, you do not think that you have a problem. Because you do not recognize the problem, whatever the illness is, you believe you are healthy and successful, and all the while you are evaluating and celebrating or perhaps bemoaning the wrong things. Because things that need correction go unaddressed, problems progress from bad to worse, and through it all everyone feels happy and content. If you knew you were deceived, you wouldn't be deceived; that's the sinister part of the problem.

Jesus concludes each of His letters with the same admonition: "He who has an ear, let him hear what the Spirit says to the churches." If we are to have any hope of transfusion, we must have an ear that wants to hear the truth even if we do not like what the Spirit has to say. Our vision will be polluted if we simply rely on our own viewpoint to assess our health and success because we are part of the problem, not the solution. Only when we are brutally honest, repent (change our mind), and seek Jesus' own viewpoint will we be able to see the truth.

COMMON AREAS OF DEPENDENCE IN CHURCHES TODAY

Let us examine some general areas where we have created a strong dependence on others rather than on Jesus.

Hearing leaders instead of God. The most obvious area of dependence that is keeping the church earthbound to its human leaders is in the area of hearing from God. For centuries now the church has been led to believe that doctrine is the means to maturity and the keepers of the doctrine are the teachers. For many, if not most, Christians, they hear from God through other people's messages packaged in sermons, books, blogs, or podcasts. It is quite common for someone to say, "When I read the Bible myself, it doesn't make sense, but when I hear my pastor speak, it comes alive for me." This is a clear indication of a dependence issue. God doesn't need a human translator. He doesn't have a difficult time communicating. The problem is that we are not hearing well.

And these teachers may be interfering with our ability to hear God, as can be seen everywhere. A study Bible is half from God and the other half notes from a teacher telling us all what God really meant. A small devotional kept in the bathroom has a single page to read every day consisting of a single Bible verse, a short uplifting story, and a quip or poem at the end—all can be read in the time it takes to take care of your regular business. The plain fact is that as long as people are more inclined to hear from other people than from God, we will remain sick and dying.

Being told how to think. Closely related to their dependence on leaders for the word of God is ordinary Christians' inability to think with a spiritual worldview because they rely so much on their leaders to think for them. Fear of thinking wrongly is pervasive, and the side effect is that people are afraid of thinking for themselves for fear they will get it wrong. There are entire ministries established just to think for everyone else. People turn to these keepers of Christian thought to find out what is right and what is wrong. Can they see a Harry Potter movie? Can they read *The Da Vinci Code*? If they do, what should they think about the work afterward? All this can be done for you. You do not have to discern a cult or heresy because the Bible answer man will do that for you. This dumbs down the people of God, and they actually become even more susceptible to false teaching because they will trust anyone with a solid education, persuasive words, and denominational credentials.

Top-down planning. Closely related to the previous dependence issue is the idea that a few people hear from God and tell the rest of us what needs to be done. So many churches are waiting for Senior Pastor Moses to descend from the mountain, tablets in hand, to tell them what God's plan is for the church in the next year. We all hear what God wants to do through the senior pastor and then try and figure out how we best fit into that plan. There is no room in the church for ordinary Christians to hear from God and go out and obey what they hear without first checking to see if or where it fits in with the master plan. We are so bound to the "master plan" that we have missed the Master's plan.

Expecting others to carry the kingdom. Ministry is something done in and by a church, so ordinary Christians do not think it is up to them to bring the influence of the kingdom with them at work, on campus, or in their neighborhood. Oh, for sure we encourage them to be a witness there, but as far as actually establishing the reign of Christ in these places, our people are woefully unprepared. They don't even think it's their job. Why? Because that task is reserved for official church ministries to do. For some strange reason we tend to think that any real influence in the world must have some ministry brand attached to it or it isn't legit. Hogwash! In fact, every Christian should be having influence in the world, and the only brand needed is the name of Christ.

Being financially dependent. This dependence goes both ways. The leaders depend on the church people for financial security, but the people that are served by the money also depend on it. Leaders who depend on the "institution" for their livelihood are bound by its obvious walls of constraint and conformity. Wherever money is needed and acquired you will find dependence, politics, temptations, and self-serving. In our real world this is unavoidable, but perhaps we have accepted it all a little too easily when it comes to church.

It is a challenge to get people dependent on the institution to do anything contrary to its success. As Upton Sinclair once quipped, "It is difficult to get a man to understand something, when his salary depends upon his not understanding it!"[1] The result of this is that the individuals who are more likely to be able to change the institution have the least motivation to change it.

Another aspect of this financial arrangement is that people who are served by the church's ministry often feel inadequate to multiply that ministry because it costs too much. This is even more evident in cross-cultural missions where a people are reached by Western missionaries. Those who are converted by the message of the missionaries are not inclined to pass the message on because they cannot emulate the expensive model of most missionary endeavors.

There is wisdom behind Jesus' advice to "carry no money belt" when he sent out the disciples (Luke 10:4). People who have heard the gospel from the disciples who arrive without any financial backing have no qualms about passing the message on to the next tribe or village because it obviously doesn't cost tons of U.S. dollars. In some of the worst cases today, we pay national leaders to serve their own people with U.S. dollars, creating a strong sense of dependence on the Western church. In such cases the national church will never flourish indigenously because there is too much dependence on the outside for success.

This is a tempting method for U.S. mission agencies, however. People can support full-time church planters in some nations for the simple cost of giving up a latte every day. We are a wealthy nation, so it feels good to share that wealth and reach other people for Christ. This method appeals to our heart and our bottom line. There is the promise of dozens and in some cases hundreds or even thousands of churches started this way. But while the initial cost to the mission agencies is low, the ultimate cost to the reproductive effectiveness of the indigenous church is quite high because it creates a permanent dependence that is almost impossible to break as time goes on.

The national leaders will never be able to raise support levels from their own people to maintain the status they receive from U.S. ministry pay, so they just continue looking for more U.S. donors to subsidize their ministry. In some cases there are church planter brokers who will promise more churches planted to U.S. foundations for a certain price. This will never reproduce. Some will counter: "But we have started tens of thousands of churches this way so it is obviously reproducing and successful." Our response is: "Stop paying money today and see what is left behind tomorrow. Until you do that you will not be able to discern what real fruit you are seeing."

This method skewers the motivations of emerging national leaders who find that being a pastor pays better than any other potential vocation. Those leaders also find that their lifestyle under U.S. support is elevated above their relational levels of influence, so their ministry, while far more expensive, is also less effective. All of this creates an unhealthy and dysfunctional dependence and damages the effectiveness of the indigenous church. There are many stories of this method ruining any hope of movements being ignited among indigenous groups.

STARTING THE DETOX PROCESS

If our description of the dependence problem rings true for you and you are willing to admit your role in perpetuating it, now is the time to stop. Consider this an intervention! As Chip and Dan Heath wrote in their best-selling book *Switch: How to Change Things*

When Change Is Hard, "All change efforts have something in common: for anything to change someone has to start acting differently."[2] It is time for leadership to start acting differently. Here are a few suggestions.

STOP BEING THE BIBLE ANSWER MAN

It goes against all our training and education as pastors, but stop being the one with all the answers. Become the one with all the good questions. Point people to the Bible instead of to yourself. It dawned on me (Neil) one day as I was reading my Bible that the one who asks the most questions in the Bible is the one who has all the answers—God. You do not have to go very far before the questions start pouring out. By chapter 3 you have "Adam, where are you?" "Who told you that you were naked? Did you eat of the fruit I told you not to eat from?" Jesus was constantly asking questions. In fact, He often answered a question with a question.

I was once in church when a young man asked a good question for which I had a great answer. Before I could speak, however, I felt the Holy Spirit tell me to hush and try something else. So I said, "That's a great question. Why don't we pray and ask the Lord for a good answer." We prayed and sat in silence for a few moments. Then I asked, "Did anyone hear any good answers from the Holy Spirit?" It amazed me how people shared Scripture that came to their minds, and I found that their answers—actually, God's answers—were better than mine.

Another time among this same spiritual family we had a rather outspoken guest who was more than delighted to share his opinions generously during our Bible discussion time. Unfortunately, he taught something that was heretical—a works-based righteousness. I took issue with this and was about to rebut him when the same internal voice told me to hush again. Instead I asked the group, "What do you guys think of what he just shared?" I was blessed and amazed to watch the body itself correct false doctrine.

In both of these examples, instead of being the source of all the right answers, I showed the people that they were connected to the Source. They learned that they could find an answer whether I was there or not.

Unfortunately, all too often a pastor will use the Bible to establish his or her own authority as an expert. In so doing, such leaders separate God's people from God's Word and insert themselves as the ones with all the answers. The authority should rest in the Bible, not in the teacher. Do not use the Bible to exalt yourself at the expense of others, but rather build up others (2 Cor. 10:8). Let God's authority use you for His glory and purpose, rather than the other way around.

Giving answers is easy; asking good questions is the real skill. Learn to be a good question asker. Become the Bible question man and see what happens.

Redefine the Gift of Teacher

I (Neil) used to think that the gifted teacher was the bottleneck to all multiplication because people tend to flock to good teachers to learn from them. The people never feel adequate to teach themselves when compared to the great teacher's ability. That stops multiplication dead in its tracks.

I hate to admit this, but early in my church planting, I intentionally dumbed down my teaching so that we could experience multiplication. This is foolish and only results in multiplying stupidity. It is saying, "No thanks," to God's precious gift. So I quickly stopped this practice, but the solution to the phenomenon of the teaching gift in a multiplication movement eluded me—until I found the solution while studying Ephesians 4:11–16, which says:

> And He gave some as apostles, and some as prophets, and some as evangelists, and some as pastors and teachers, for the equipping of the saints for the work of service, to the building up of the body of Christ; until we all attain to the unity of the faith, and of the knowledge of the Son of God, to a mature man, to the measure of the stature which belongs to the fullness of Christ. As a result, we are no longer to be children, tossed here and there by waves and carried about by every wind of doctrine, by the trickery of men, by craftiness in deceitful scheming; but speaking the truth in love, we are to grow up in all aspects into Him who is the head, even Christ, from whom the whole body, being fitted and held together by that which every joint supplies, according to the proper working of each individual part, causes the growth of the body for the building up of itself in love.

I realized that these influential gifts were given to the church, not to do the ministry but to equip the saints to do the ministry. So if we follow the logic, the evangelist is not called to win lost people to Christ, as we have all supposed, but rather to equip the Christians to lead lost people to Christ. In the same way, the teacher is not called to teach the saints but to equip the saints to teach others. This is how we remain steadfast in doctrine and not easily led astray: not by the great teaching of a few exceptional teachers but by the people themselves being prepared as teachers. That is when the whole body is fitted and held together by what each part contributes. This passage speaks directly against creating dependence in anyone other than Christ, the Head of the church.

If that is so, is there any place in the Bible where all Christians are told to teach? Yes, actually there are several such places, as you will soon see. Nevertheless, whenever I ask an audience if there is any command for all Christians to teach, the overwhelming majority of people answer in the negative. Why is that? We believe it is because they have been trained to think that way by centuries of poor practices reinforcing an unhealthy dependence on a few teachers.

First, Colossians 3:16 exhorts us all to teach one another. We are all to let the Word of Christ richly dwell within us, and the result is that we will teach one another.

Second, the Great Commission is to make disciples by "teaching them to obey" all that Christ commanded. That command is given to us all by Jesus and states beforehand that He has all authority of heaven and earth. We think that is both clear and compelling.

Third, 1 Corinthians 14:26 describes church gatherings as places where "each one has a psalm, has a teaching, has a revelation, has a tongue, has an interpretation. Let all things be done for edification."

Finally, the writer of Hebrews wrote:

Concerning Him [Christ] we have much to say, and it is hard to explain, since you have become dull of hearing. For though by this time you ought to be teachers, you have need again for someone to teach you the elementary principles of the oracles of God, and you have come to need milk and not solid food. For everyone who partakes only of milk is not accustomed to the word of righteousness, for he is an infant. [Heb. 5:11–14]

It clearly says that by now all of the Hebrew Christians should be teachers, but unfortunately they had become "dull of hearing" and could not handle the meat of God's Word but merely the milk. What is milk? Our mentor and teacher, Harold Dunning, used to say that milk is "predigested food." Think about it. The mother eats the food, it is digested, and the nutrients are absorbed and then passed on to the baby as milk. In other words, milk is a sermon. A sermon is predigested meat (the word of righteousness), consumed by the pastor and then fed to the flock.

How often have we heard people say they were leaving a church because they just weren't getting fed there? For far too long we have lived with this dysfunctional codependent relationship that expects the pastor to feed us. Since when does a shepherd feed his sheep? Sheep feed themselves! A good shepherd leads his flock to green pastures and still waters, but he doesn't open the sheep's mouth and stick a handful of grass in it.[3]

There is a time when shepherds feed their sheep: when they are orphaned lambs. And in that case they feed them with a bottle of milk. We can never expect our church to mature into the image of Christ if we allow them to remain babies who are stuck sucking milk from their pastor week after week.

With this in mind, I have taken to evaluating the gifted teacher in a new way. Getting the message right is only a quarter of the task. Communicating the message so that others understand the content only brings the teacher to half of his or her role. Seeing the content applied well in the listener's context is another 25 percent of the task of the teacher but still only brings the teacher to 75 percent fulfillment. Seventy-five percent on an exam is barely passing and certainly not considered a success. The teacher is completely successful only when the people they teach can and do teach others. Releasing the learners to fulfill the task of the teacher themselves with other people is the only way a teacher can fulfill 100 percent of his or her call. It is also the only way that the role of the teacher can be a catalyst for multiplication rather than a barrier to the same.

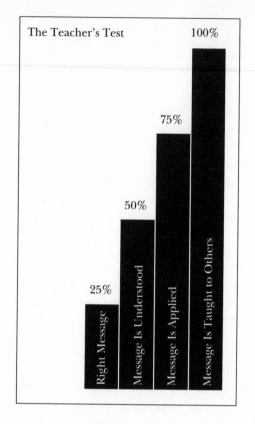

We need to redefine what it means to teach. It is not simply passing on content to others. We prefer to see teaching as facilitating the learning of others so that they know, do, and pass on to others the relevant and meaningful truth.

A couple of suggestions for the teachers out there: never teach a second lesson until the first one is done. A lesson is not done until it is being passed on. What would the kingdom of God look like if we had more teachers like this?

All of us who have fulfilled the role of teacher are aware that we learn so much more by teaching than we ever did by being taught. In fact, one of the most frustrating realities of teaching is that you are not able to convey to the people all that you

have been able to learn. There is good reason for this. It is
God's design for teachers to teach people to become teachers,
for then people will learn the truths of God's Word on much
deeper levels.

This pedagogy has many benefits:

- The people learn the truth on a far deeper level.
- The people understand and own the truth rather than merely
  remember it.
- The people are held to greater accountability to practice the
  truth they learned.
- The people own the message rather than simply know it.

When you take a test, you reveal what you remember from
someone's teaching. When you practice what you have heard, you
demonstrate that your will is now involved in the learning process
because you are choosing to obey the message and thus you have
taken it in more deeply. When you start to teach the subject to
others, you have to reconcile the logic behind the facts and not
just remember the facts themselves.

When you pass the lessons on to others, you demonstrate a
greater level of ownership. Isn't that what we want? We do not
want people who know facts about the gospel but rather people
who apply them and then own them in the depth of their
soul. We do not want only an audience or even practitioners; we
want agents of the gospel. Change is not enough; we want change
agents.

At CMA we have developed a learning system for systematic
theology based on this type of thinking. It is a one-year learning
process for proven leaders during which they learn theology in a
small community by teaching it in a highly reproducible manner.
It is called TruthQuest and is available on our Web site.[4] Each
learning community consists of between four and eight people,
all of whom have two systematic theology textbooks, and no two
people have the same two textbooks. For about a year, the group
meets once a month on a Saturday for about eight hours, with
three breaks.[5] At each meeting the group members are called on
randomly to teach the rest of the group a portion of what they

learned while studying the Bible and their textbooks on the particular doctrine being examined that month. After one has spoken, the others are called on to challenge or add to what was taught. After the theological discussion, each learner must apply the doctrine in a practical way to the DNA of his or her own life, preferably with a story or an example. At the end of the year, all the learners in the group are capable of leading another group through the process. TruthQuest is not a curriculum and will not teach you what to think but rather how to think. The participants may not come out thinking the same as you, but they will come out able to think for themselves. We value a person's ability to think clearly and logically even more than having that person simply agree with us.

Over the years we have found that individuals trained in this manner who then went through our denomination's licensure process[6] are even better than many who come with seminary education at not only understanding the concepts and doctrines but also at defending them with the Scripture. They can also explain the variety of positions that exist on a particular subject and explain why they have chosen what they believe. If the goal of training is credentialing people who know "the right answers," this system will not work, but if your goal is to create a thirst for learning and give them the tools to think and learn for themselves, then TruthQuest is a great tool.

STOP OPERATING WITH POSITIONAL AUTHORITY

There are different kinds of authority. You have positional authority when your position or role (as pastor, for example) is the source of your power and influence. We strongly suggest that you no longer use positional authority—no matter how high your rank—to get things done. Spiritual and relational authority are far superior anyway, so use them to get work done. The Pharisees and Sadducees had all the positional authority and Jesus had none. But after the Sermon on the Mount, Matthew writes, "When Jesus had finished these words, the crowds were amazed at His teaching; for He was teaching them as one having authority, and not as their scribes" (Matt. 7:28–29).

If you can't get things done without positional authority, you do not deserve the position in the first place. If you can get things done without using your position, you are truly beginning to lead and not just manage.

We will speak more on this issue in Chapter Eight.

Learn to Become a Disposable Pastor

Reading the *Los Angeles Times* on July 4, 2011, I (Neil) was struck by the contrast between two separate articles. The first article was about some retired citizens in Japan that have formed a team called the Skilled Veterans Corps.[7] The team volunteered to enter the Fukushima nuclear power plant to perform necessary repairs to the damage caused by the tsunami and subsequent meltdown so that younger workers did not have to. The youngest on this corps is sixty and the oldest is seventy-eight. These are real heroes. The article explained that they recognize they do not have as long to live as the younger generation and they feel some responsibility because they have benefited from nuclear power for a longer period of time. They add that since their own cells reproduce at a slower pace, they would take longer to contract cancer and die from it and likely will die sooner anyway. The truth is, they are willing to sacrifice their own lives so that their children and grandchildren do not have to. The Web site calling for volunteers states, "This is our duty to the next generation and the one thereafter."

The second article reported that the Rev. Robert H. Schuller had allegedly been voted off the board of directors of the Crystal Cathedral.[8] Later, the church released a statement that he was not voted off the board, though he is no longer a voting member. Of note is that it was Schuller's son (who was ousted from the church a few years ago) who made the original comment, indicating that there is still plenty of drama at the Crystal Cathedral even without the legendary Christmas pageant.

Just as this church was a forerunner in the megachurch phenomenon, in my own opinion it is heralding a coming problem that the American megachurch must address soon. A few years ago, Schuller retired and left the church in the hands of his son. Not long after that, his son was fired and his daughter was placed in charge. The church has plummeted in attendance to the point where it found it difficult for years to get a shot of the audience for the TV show because there were so many empty seats. Even more striking than the low attendance are the high debt and lack of financial resources. The church went into bankruptcy and has now sold its famous property to the Catholic church.

So what do these two articles have in common? The answer is retiring leadership that is responsible for releasing the next generation. In one case the fathers respond with heroic sacrifice for the sake of their children and grandchildren. In the other case the senior leadership does not adequately prepare the next generation and leaves a sinking ship in the hands of siblings in conflict while their aging father continues to grasp at what power he can until he is finally forced out.

Most megachurches in America are still led by their dynamic founding pastors, who are getting older and in many cases have passed retirement age but still continue leading as if they were immortal. They are not, and if they do not raise up the next generation and hand off the baton properly, they too will see their ministry shrivel up and die like the Crystal Cathedral's.

Many of these dynamic senior leaders have children who have grown into leaders themselves, much like Schuller. While some have done well at releasing their offspring, others are not doing as well. It is frankly a bit shocking that so many leaders have their sons take their place, like some sort of monarchy or family-owned business. Billy Graham has Franklin step into his shoes. Jerry Falwell is replaced by his son. Charles Stanley's influence is now eclipsed by Andy, even though it wasn't always a smooth transition. Many of these successions have not gone well, as the Schuller debacle glaringly demonstrates.

To their credit, these leaders have raised children who are following the Lord and leading in the church, and for that we should give honor. But the issue is that our approach to doing church is not efficient at passing the baton to the next generation. The sort of leader who can build a megachurch is not the sort of leader who is good at giving away the ministry to others, and therein lies the problem.

The real issue is that the leadership of the previous generation is holding on for too long. The famous teachers are not producing the next generation of teachers but instead are holding on to the influence, which creates a dependence that does not reproduce. The pastor who is the centerpiece of an attractional model tends to become invaluable and irreplaceable. Those leaders, likely doing it all for good reasons, become the linchpins of success and as such ironically become a major ingredient in a church's ultimate demise.

We believe that the megachurch of today is far more vulnerable than it appears to be. Dependence on a specific charismatic leader and the funds that such a leader draws is actually very crippling and will likely implode in many cases.

One remarkable passage that we may have read dozens of times but not really considered in light of today's church leadership is a simple statement by Paul in his epistle to the Philippians (2:12–13). He says:

> So then, my beloved, just as you have always obeyed, not as in my presence only, but now much more in my absence, work out your salvation with fear and trembling; for it is God who is at work in you, both to will and to work for His good pleasure.

We are familiar with these words and have perhaps even preached, heard, or read messages about working out your own salvation and what that means. But how many of us took the time to consider the opening statement that this church was actually doing better in Paul's absence than in his presence? That, friends, is a huge statement and perhaps even an indictment against the current expressions of leadership found in most of our churches.

We do not need a succession plan as if the current leaders are so valuable that we must spend hours or even days trying to figure out how to replace them with other dynamic leaders who are equally valuable and consequently equally vulnerable. What we need is a leader with a heart of sacrifice who is more concerned with his or her spiritual children's success than with his or her own and will lead in such a way that others are empowered to do even better than the previous leader. What we need is sacrifice rather than succession, like those fathers in Japan.

Draw up an exit plan in the next few days that gives away your ministry to your spiritual children, and put it to use. Become a disposable pastor. You will find that disposable pastors actually become more valuable, not less, because they are few and more needed.

I (Neil) have seen my role as a pastor change from being valuable to being disposable. Instead of being needed, I want to be forgotten. I consider myself a success when I can fade from the picture and allow others to be empowered and to rise to the job before us. This is the true calling of a leader in God's kingdom. The one who wants to be great is a servant of all. This is the difference between being a doer and being an equipper.

When you exist to help others do the job in your stead, you have matured to the level of an equipper. The more valuable you are, the less successful you are as an equipper of others. Ironically, the more disposable you become, the more valuable you truly are, because there are not that many leaders today who are able or willing to do this. We have entered the era of recyclable disciples and disposable pastors. If you are not willing to give your role to someone else, you do not deserve the role. As a leader in God's kingdom, your success is no longer to be evaluated by what you do but by what others around you are able to do. You cannot get to the place where you see your life and ministry this way without taking the lonely road through the cross. A crucified leader is an equipper of others.

The best exit strategy as a leader in a ministry is a sound empowerment strategy. If you are unable to empower others to do the job, you will never be able to leave well.

Detox is a chance for a clean start. Before you start, you need to settle your own identity issues as a pastor or Christian leader, or you will simply create the same problems all over again. You can count on the fact that what is good for your ego is not good for the kingdom. Conversely, what is hard on your ego can often be good for the kingdom. John the Baptist figured this out and remarked, "I must decrease and He must increase" (John 3:30). Every pastor needs to come to a similar conclusion.

In Chapter Seven we address how small-minded leaders can cause big problems and suggest that finding your identity in Christ as a leader is most essential to instigating a transfusion of organic life in a church.

HOW SMALL PEOPLE
CAUSE BIG PROBLEMS

In my book *Organic Leadership*, I (Neil) tell a story of General William Winder, a U.S. brigadier general during the War of 1812.[1] This story bears repeating.

During one battle he had a four-to-one troop advantage over the British and still lost the fight. He was captured, but the British realized in a stroke of genius that thanks to his ineptness, he was of better use to them free than imprisoned, so they let him go!

This genius was proved one year later when the Brits overcame our defenses, led by General Winder, and took our nation's capital. The Union Jack flew over our Capitol building where the Stars and Stripes should have been.

It is a tragedy when a leader finds that he is actually more valuable to the enemy's cause than his own. General Winder was not intentionally trying to sabotage his own cause. I believe his incompetence and inadvertent assistance to the opposition was purely a result of personal inadequacies that leaked out on to the battlefield. Bad leaders with good motives are still bad leaders. Unfortunately, I believe that many leaders in today's church may suffer from a fate similar to General Winder's.

In this chapter we look at what can cause a leader with good intentions to benefit the enemy's cause more than his or her own. Until we become leaders who participate in the advancement of the kingdom, we are wasting time with other concerns. In this chapter we will unmask a character flaw that tends to cause more damage than good to the church, and we will also explain how to uproot this flaw. In a sense, before we can talk about actions that can cause good things for the church, we need to address the behavior that causes harm. Then we can address the things that will bring health and fruitfulness.

The Source of Smallness in a Person's Life

A great many character flaws can betray a leader. Pride, anger, greed, and lust all have a hand in the self-destruction of many leaders. In our experience, however, we have found that insecurity is the root cause that tends to fuel many other character faults. Insecurity makes us smaller people, but leads us to make decisions that cause big problems.

Insecurity is a common problem; in fact, everyone struggles with it in one way or another. We all seem to start from a place of insecurity for one very good reason: we were meant for glory and now live in a fallen world. None of us have lived up to the promise of creation, and we all know it deep in our hearts. We can blame Adam and Eve, we can blame our parents or the government, but the truth we all know in our hearts is that each of us carry guilt and shame for our own sins in this fallen world. None of us have lived up to our great potential and carry within us every day the shame of expectations that have not been met—expectations from God, our fellow humans, and ourselves.

An Equal-Opportunity Condition

On TV a supermodel described her insecurity in this way. She had built her own bathroom with mirrors surrounding her. Now that sounds egotistical and vain, doesn't it? It probably is. But she went on to note that having mirrors all around her caused her to continually notice the dimples in her butt. Is it possible that someone as prideful as a supermodel who is seen adorning the covers of magazines at every checkout line in the world and who surrounds herself with mirrors could be insecure? The most beautiful people in the world look into the mirror and see the flaws that likely only they can find. They know that the airbrush covers the imperfections that might otherwise be evident. They know that age will steal from them their greatest asset, and this insecurity drives them.

The most successful people in the world hide their insecurity behind their ambition and pride, but they fear that one day everyone will find out that they do not really deserve the success they have achieved. This compels them to strive even harder for success and acceptance, often striving to convince themselves, as much as anyone else, that they really do deserve the success they protect. Kings build elaborate palaces because they fear they will be forgotten in time. They want to prove to the world and to themselves that they are worthy of their success, but it never truly feels that way. What we see as ego is often a broken person striving to be important but feeling inside that he or she fails to live up to appearances. Of course, such people feel they are better than others—that is their "reward" for working so hard to overcome their insecurity—but they still do not feel that they are good enough. Prostitutes toss themselves away because they fear they are not worthy of anything else. The farther down the path of self-destruction the prostitute goes, the less she feels worthy of love and value, so she sells herself for less. In each of these cases, it is insecurity that drives them, and each one ends up selling their goodness because they do not feel valuable or content with who they are.

It is hard to imagine that the most powerful and successful people in the world suffer from the same sense of inferiority as some of the most broken and trampled on, but we believe it is true. Insecurity motivates them both in seemingly opposite directions. As these broken people progress in each direction, insecurity speeds their destruction. Successful individuals see all that they have accomplished and realize that they have much to lose if people ever wake up and realize that they don't deserve their success, so they are compelled by that same insecurity to do some pretty ugly things to protect what they have and fear they may lose. The lowly feel less valued with each decision of self-destruction. As a result, they have no resistance to giving themselves even further to the destruction because they do not feel that they are worth much anyway—and less and less with each self-destructive step.

The problem isn't whether we have insecurities or not. We all do. The problem is that we let those insecurities rule our lives. That is what causes many leaders to become more of a problem than a solution in Christ's cause. Insecurity can lead us to make foolish decisions, which can leave us full of ego or full of self-defeat; either direction is destructive and helps the enemy's cause more than our own.

Let's look at a biblical story of a man who was driven by insecurity and see how it can lead to some incredibly foolish decisions that affect others and, like General Winder, can leave a person fighting on the wrong side of his own cause.

THE STORY OF JOHN, THE SON OF ZEBEDEE

We are accustomed to hearing about Peter's big mistakes with Jesus in the gospels, but I believe that John also made many missteps. He too needed to be forgiven and restored.

Imagine what life would be like if you were a fisherman on the Sea of Galilee in the first century. Your life would consist of hours spent on the water, hauling in nets, cleaning fish, and repairing nets, and then hawking your catch at the local market. Day in and day out, you would smell of fish. You would have the worn hands of a man who hauled heavy nets, rowed oars, and trimmed sails every day.

A fisherman's livelihood depends on the grace of God providing a good wind and a good catch. Some days are better than others. Some seasons are better than others. This was John's life, and his hopes and dreams were built on finding a good spouse and raising a family so that his children could carry on the family's business when his own body could no longer lift the weight of the fish-laden nets.

Such a fisherman likely had no ambition beyond these simple things. He never considered travel beyond the annual pilgrimage to Jerusalem. He would never aspire to further his education or to write a book. He was invested in a trade that would demand that he set sail every day but Saturday. Other ambitions would not be possible.

Then one day John had the best catch of his entire life, of anyone's life actually—a seeming world record number of fish miraculously caught. What is remarkable is this is the second most important news to alter his life on that afternoon. The first thing was that an up-and-coming rabbi with seemingly miraculous power challenged John and his brother James to become His disciples.

All of us remember what it is like to wait to be chosen to play on the schoolyard team. Many of us know what it is like not to be selected at all. Being chosen first, second, or third was always a boost to our ego even if we were struggling with internal insecurity. One night Jesus went up on the mountain to pray and returned prepared to select his team—and John's name was called third! Imagine how unlikely this must have seemed for a Galilean fisherman and his brother. One day your biggest concern was mending nets, and the next day you are an apprentice of a great rabbi. Jesus selected twelve men, but John was the third name called, and that must have been one of the best moments of his life. But things were about to get even better.

Jesus granted authority to the twelve and sent them out to heal and cast out demons. One day John was cleaning fish, now he was cleansing lepers and souls of demonic influence.

Then John was asked to join Jesus and Peter and James. They went up on a hill, and Jesus began to glow in the dark. John found himself in unique company, to say the least, for he was in a small band of men that included the Messiah, Moses, and Elijah! All his life he had heard of Moses and Elijah. He'd heard the stories; now here he was with them. How that must have played tricks with his ego! All the holy religious leaders of past centuries, even the legendary ones, were not chosen to be in this company, yet John was.

John made the first cut to be one of the twelve. Then he made the second cut to be one of the three. We imagine that as the sons of Zebedee were descending the mountaintop, they felt there must have been one more cut coming—and that they had an advantage over the other guy. They were two brothers against just one Peter. They wanted to come out on top.

Maybe they wondered how they could approach Jesus with such an ambitious request. By this time they had spent enough time with Jesus to know that he would not take kindly to selfish ambition. They couldn't just ask for themselves. They couldn't expect any of the other disciples to make the request for them. Whom could they get to lobby on their behalf? Perhaps in hindsight it wasn't a good idea, but they knew they could always count on good old mom.

We don't know John and James' mother's name (they are called the Sons of Thunder, so we wonder if that makes her Thunder), but she came to Jesus with a strange request. She said, "I want you to do whatever I ask of you." That is a bold proclamation to make to the Lord of Lords and King of Kings, but there is nothing like a motivated mother.

Jesus, always the servant, asked her what she wanted, and she replied that she wanted her boys to sit in His kingdom, one on His right and one on His left. This would make them His number one and number two men. Jesus did something unusual at this point. He could have said, "No, that's not how it works in My kingdom." But He didn't. Instead, He turned to the boys and asked them a question: "Are you willing to pay the price?"—to which they both responded in the affirmative.

We imagine that they felt at that moment that their hopes were about to be realized. For why else would Jesus ask such a question? They likely expected Him to ask them to raise their right hands and repeat an oath, but that is not at all what happened. Jesus elevated their expectations with His question and at the same time raised their level of accountability. Then He brought them back down to reality.

Jesus told James and John that they would indeed pay that price but that to guarantee them such a position in His kingdom was not within His authority. "Huh?" they must have thought. He set them up big time! Why? He was teaching them a lesson that was very important. This is a lesson He needs us all to learn, and sometimes He needs to shake us up in order to teach us. In fact, even this dramatic lesson was not enough for John and his brother, but it was a start.

A wrong view of the kingdom always leads to selfish ambition and striving to be over others, but it is wrong and is usually a product of insecurity. Jesus cannot say it more emphatically than He did in the gospels; nevertheless, we still get it wrong. His kingdom is not of the world. Authority in God's kingdom doesn't operate the same way it does in the world. John didn't understand this, and Jesus needed to get his attention to teach him this lesson. I believe this is why Jesus set the boys up for a huge disappointment, so that they would be open to learning one of the most important lessons of their lives. And it's a lesson they would pay the ultimate price to learn.

Until this moment everything seemed to be going John's way. He must have felt that he couldn't fail. The thing about insecurity is that even when all seems to be going right, it is still inside us. When Jesus rebuked him in a very deliberate and humiliating manner, I imagine that John began to wonder if he might not only be rejected for the position he sought but also lose the one he already had. That's the problem with success: you gain something you can lose. If John had never met Jesus, he would likely be content with life as usual and never have given position and success a second thought, but not so now. Since he had walked with Jesus, seen the miracles, performed the miracles, and now even been in the company of Moses and Elijah, he had much to lose, and that weighed heavily on his heart when he found himself on the wrong end of a rebuke from Jesus.

But Jesus, if He is anything, is forgiving, so John likely tried to shrug off the fears and keep moving forward. But John's embarrassment was just beginning, and his feelings of insecurity and fear would continue to grow.

Soon the Sons of Thunder found that they were at odds with the other ten disciples, who likely all wanted the same position that the brothers went after. Jesus could not let this develop into an outright division in the group, so He stepped in to address it without delay. The manner in which he addressed it, however, once again stung John's ego.

Jesus took an unknown child and sat the boy on his right side and spoke about who was truly the greatest in the kingdom. In so doing He said that a small child is greatest in the kingdom and that all should become like this child. What is remarkable in context is that Jesus intentionally placed a small, know-nothing boy in the very spot where John was hoping to be seated. He did this in front of all the other disciples while they were discussing who was greatest among them in response to John's ambitious request. Do not miss the significant humiliation John would have felt at this moment. Jesus not only said no to John's request, but then while the disciples were discussing who is greatest, He promoted a small boy to the place John wished to be. This must have devastated John in front of his peers. This is when we believe John's insecurity began to drive his actions in destructive ways.

Insecurity tends to feed on ego-driven action, but the fear inside is never satisfied. As John's fears begin to build, his actions dramatically betray his insecurity.

Next the boys approach Jesus with a report about a stranger casting out demons in Jesus' name without permission. In doing so, they were demonstrating not only that they were taking initiative in the use of the authority Jesus had given them but also that they were trying diligently to remain in His good graces and part of the inner circle.

John said, "Master, we saw someone casting out demons in your name; and we tried to prevent him because he does not follow along with us." This report was a poorly veiled attempt to assure themselves that they were part of the special inner circle and that others were not. In their words there is a sharp contrast between *someone* and *us* because they wanted Jesus to be reminded that they were some of his most trusted followers and not just some stranger off the street. But Jesus' answer did not provide them with the assurance they had hoped for. Instead of confirming their place in the inner circle, He questioned their action, saying, "Do not hinder him; for anyone who is not against you is for you."

That was what Jesus said, but this is what John and James probably heard: "He is not against us; therefore, he is one of us, as much as you are." Suddenly, little boys and strangers were just as important as John and his brother. Their fear is beginning to consume them.

Instead of providing the assurance they had desired, this answer only inflamed their own sense of insecurity. They felt they were losing something very important, and they needed to do something quick, decisive, and bold to regain their place. But what could they do? They needed to do something to remind Jesus of how special they were and at the same time not provoke Jesus to include some other stranger as their previous actions had done. Jesus made it clear that if someone is not against Him, they are for Him, so they began looking for someone, anyone, who could be considered against Him. They did not have to wait long.

On their way to Jerusalem the band attempted to find lodging at an inn in Samaria. The fact that Jesus and his disciples regularly passed through Samaria was unusual. Most of the Jews in the north would travel many miles out of the way to avoid setting foot in that region because Samaritans were considered unclean people. This attitude was never lost on the Samaritans, who likely resented the prejudice. Perhaps this is the reason that there was no room in the inn for Jesus and His disciples. Interesting, isn't it? How there never seems to be room at the inn for Jesus.

As they were getting ready to carry on with the journey, the Sons of Thunder thought this was their moment to prove themselves to Jesus. They had likely been looking for just the right opportunity. It had to be someone whom Jesus wouldn't promote to their position as He did with the boy or the stranger who was performing exorcisms. Surely a Samaritan would fit the profile. It also had to be someone who is not "for us" but obviously "against us," and those who would not even offer them shelter were surely against them.

Hearing the response from the Samaritan innkeeper, James and John said, "Lord, do You want us to command fire to come down from heaven and consume them?" Wow, what a response. We read this and see its stupidity, but somehow they thought it an appropriate response. Why? How?

Insecurity. Fear was eating away at their sense of value in the eyes of Jesus. They could remember the high points—being selected among the twelve and then as one of the three, being granted authority over demons and sickness, being in the small band with Moses and Elijah and seeing a part of Jesus even the other nine disciples did not have the privilege to see. But they could also remember all the rebukes since then—the setup and slam-down for aspiring to be first and second, the embarrassing rebuke in front of their peers by placing a boy in their desired spot, the rebuke for hindering a rogue exorcist who wasn't one of the chosen few.

They wanted to remind Jesus of the height of their advancement, the peak of their experience on the mountaintop beside Moses and Elijah, and so to remind Him of this moment they decided to exercise the kind of power that only someone in that circle could do. Surely the other ten disciples wouldn't try this. They asked if they should do what only Elijah had ever done, command fire to fall from heaven and consume His opponents. In their minds I imagine this all made sense. But as we read the story, it makes no sense at all. That's the problem with insecurity; it takes you down a path that leads to deception and foolishness. Objectivity is lost in the mire of irrational fear.

I try to imagine the look on Jesus' face at this moment. It is hard to surprise Jesus, but I cannot imagine that He expected such a fearful and insecure response. I think he turned, looked at them in wonder, and said, "You do not know what kind of spirit you are of; for the Son of Man did not come to destroy men's lives but to save them." He knew that their reaction was not of the Spirit that comes from God. It was fleshly, egotistical, and motivated by fear. (And it is this sort of motivation that can cause a leader to do more harm than good in the church.) Jesus strongly rebuked them and let them know that the two of them were as much against Jesus as any Samaritan innkeeper.

I can almost feel the heat emanating from their red faces at this most embarrassing of moments. What they had hoped would regain them favor with Jesus actually became the worst nightmare they could have imagined. At this point the Zebedee boys were likely deflated and resigned to remaining mostly quiet. Every step they had taken to try to get back on top had seemingly knocked them farther down the ladder. Of course, the real problem is that there was no ladder to begin with and Jesus was trying to tell them this, but in their insecure frame of mind, they couldn't hear it. They were probably so defeated that they hung their heads, dragged their feet, and were filled with self-loathing and shame.

The next time we get a glimpse of John, he is resting his head on Jesus at the Last Supper. He is not speaking many words or doing much to try and prove his position; instead he appears to have moved toward relational intimacy, which is probably a wise decision.

The hopes of James and John must have been lifted a bit when Jesus requested that they join Him and Peter in prayer in the Garden of Gethsemane. Is this a second chance? Were they wondering if they were still in the inner circle in spite of all of their mistakes? I wonder how the other nine felt at that moment. I also wonder what the three who had been invited were expecting when they accompanied Jesus into a very private and intimate moment. Did they expect Jesus to glow in the dark again? Did they anticipate meeting up with some other important historical figure or to hang out with Moses and Elijah again?

But this moment was different from that previous mountain-top experience, and that was evident right away. Jesus' mood was far more melancholy. When it became clear that they were only to be there while He prayed and there would be no grand event, their bodies lost all adrenaline and they relaxed—into a coma! Luke mentions that they were so tired because of sorrow. They reflected the pain and sorrow that Jesus felt but also, perhaps, some regret. At this point James and John as well as Peter had all done some pretty stupid things that may have caused them to be full of regret and sorrow. They did not understand all that was taking place. As a result, they fell asleep, and Jesus rebuked them twice, which likely stirred up that insecurity again.

This is a significant moment in human history, and with front-row seats, the boys take a nap. It is rare for Jesus to ask someone to do something for His personal welfare, but at this moment He requested their solidarity in prayer. This request was met with slow, steady breathing and drooling. Jesus went to them three times to check on them, and twice he woke them with a rebuke; once he simply let them sleep.

With the insecurity swirling in their heads once again, before they even had time to consider these things, their Master was taken away for an unjust and rapid trial. John would follow at a distance but only observe. His own insecurity was now replaced with a new kind of fear. Suddenly he was less concerned about his own place in Jesus' chain of command; now it was Jesus Himself who was in danger.

John watched as Jesus was judged and sentenced to death. He followed the procession to Golgotha and remained beside the women at the foot of the cross. There, Jesus in some of His last words asked him to care for Mary, His mother, for the rest of her life. This is a solemn and final act. In this dark and deadly hour, John has lost all hope of a position in some coming kingdom. Now all he can do is show love to the one who showed only love to him. This moment was a death to his Master, a death to his ambition, a death to the life he had wanted. Everything died that day for John.

Even after encountering the risen Lord, John and his companions felt a bit lost. Their personal regrets and sorrow were not something easily abandoned. Now that Jesus had been killed and raised from the dead, what was next?

After some time in this state, they decided to go back to what they knew best: fishing. There is comfort we all find when we are involved in something familiar, something we know we can do without fear of embarrassment. When we can indulge a skill that we are actually good at, we can feel better about ourselves. I believe this was a longing that the Zebedee boys as well as Simon and Andrew were experiencing.

After a long night of catching nothing, they were probably beginning to wonder if they even knew how to fish. As they were readying to return to shore empty-handed, Jesus cried out from shore and instructed them to try dropping the nets on the other side of the boat. It was a ridiculous suggestion, but the men were accommodating and polite in spite of their fatigue. When they caught a supernatural abundance of fish reminiscent of their original call to follow Jesus, John realized who it was that gave them this instruction and mentioned it to Peter.

They hauled the miraculous load to shore only to find that Jesus had already cooked breakfast for them. He then asked Peter three times, "Simon, do you love me more than these [fish]?" Jesus was asking him if he would leave fishing forever and start shepherding Christ's people instead. Peter and the other eleven were given a fresh lease on life and a renewal of their calling in Christ. The disciples were, in a sense, recommissioned by Jesus. Just like the first time, there was a supernatural catch of fish that they would be asked to leave behind to follow Christ and fish for humanity.

Eventually, John settled his insecurity in Christ and gained a new identity, a new way of seeing himself. He wrote his gospel and uses a name for himself that we may be inclined to think is egotistical, but I believe is actually a sign of a man who has settled his insecurity. He calls himself the disciple whom Jesus loved. He who is forgiven much loves much, and John became known as the apostle of love. Leaders who are no longer insecure don't care what others think of them, even if they risk looking egotistical. What mattered to John was not others' opinions but the truth that he was loved and accepted by Jesus in spite of his poor performance and foolish actions.

The good news is that even someone who is driven by ambition and insecurity can participate in God's kingdom in a profound and lasting way. Every one of us starts with an internal insecurity that can drive us to do some stupid things. Left unaddressed, this insecurity can actually cause us to be more damaging than helpful to Christ's cause. Insecurity can drive us to jealousy, envy, pride, hatred, bigotry, lust, and just about any other darker sin, and these can cause devastating problems in the church. A leader who can help Christ's cause and bring health to the church must first be healthy. This begins with settling one's identity issues and finding security in Christ, and in Christ alone.

A leader who is no longer haunted by the fear of insecurity leads from a place of incredible strength. When one's ego is not wrapped up with performance, one will have the courage to make right decisions that may or may not be in one's own best interest. Love can flourish in a heart that finds its security and identity in Christ rather than personal performance. As the apostle of love found out, "There is no fear in love, but perfect love casts out fear."

A leader secure in his or her identity in Christ is not easily manipulated or used by the enemy. This type of leader has nothing to lose and walks with a sort of authority that is not found in titles, positions, or rank. This is a servant whom God can use to further His cause in the world.

Once you get your own identity issues straightened out, it is time to amend the way you lead others. Insecurity, as we have seen, causes a leader to do some foolish things that can be contrary to God's kingdom agenda, much like General Winder. Once you understand how secure you really are, the way you lead will begin to change. You cannot be a different person and lead effectively in the same old way. Chapter Eight addresses the important subject of how we need to change the way we lead others in the transfusion of a church.

CHAPTER EIGHT

LEADERSHIFTS

Have you ever found yourself wondering how in the world you ended up in the situation you're now in? When you first thought of entering "the ministry," you were filled with hope and passion. God was going to use you to embolden the church and change the world. That's a big goal. But we have a big God, don't we? So what happened? How did we get to the place where week after week we find ourselves exhausted from managing an organization, preaching the Word, worrying about money, dealing with whiny and selfish people, and seeing very little positive change to show for it? Is this what you signed up for?

If you find yourself in one or all of these places, we're here to help. You and your ministry can be renewed. The organic principles of life and leadership that we are sharing with you can start you on a path to recapturing the sense of meaning and purpose you once had, and they can lead you to that place of significant fruitfulness you hope for.

Part of the renewal process is to reset expectations. When I (Phil) first felt a call to ministry, I wanted nothing more than to be useful to God. I wasn't looking for any particular position, and I had no idea where to begin. I started attending Bible college and soon discovered that I could not see myself doing anything but teaching God's Word and helping God's people. But I still had no idea where to start.

As I consulted with those who had gone before me in this great enterprise, I was directed to a common path. Finish school, seek a position at a church, and start leading. So that's exactly what I did. This process was very much like any other process of preparing for a particular career and finding a place in it.

Once I found myself in a church working as a pastor, I quickly discovered that although seminary taught me theology, it did little to prepare me for church leadership. I was immediately saddled with a plethora of responsibilities and expectations that kept me very busy but left me little time to pursue my passion of helping people learn to follow Jesus. In seminary, I was taught that I should not get too close to the people (which never made any sense to me) and that if I would just preach truth on Sunday mornings, everything else would just fall into place. If it didn't, then at least I was being faithful to my calling. After all, the results were up to God.

I found myself constantly battling with this way of thinking. I worked hard to fulfill my responsibilities of managing the church and planning and executing events. But I found that without meaningful personal interactions with people who really wanted to follow Jesus, I felt empty and frustrated. Add to this well-meant criticisms of my preaching and my leadership as well as a barrage of encouragement to learn from the megachurches how to do "real" church, and I was ready for a change.

Many church leaders find themselves in a similar predicament. They often satisfy this desire for change by leaving one church and moving on to another only to find that history repeats itself. Others stay put and quietly suffer without hope.

The Great Commission is about making disciples, followers of Christ. We'll be the first to admit that our spiritual life has been profoundly influenced by great teachers of the Bible. But sermons, worship concerts, and dynamic drama presentations are a poor substitute for iron sharpening iron.

We've discovered that it's possible to get off the merry-go-round and back to the joy of our first love, making disciples. People really do want to follow Jesus. They just need someone to come alongside them and show them the way.

Leadership is really just influence of others. Much of what we find ourselves busy with is not influence but a demanding counterfeit. Management and maintenance of the organization sucks all the time, energy, and enthusiasm out of our role in the church.

Albert Einstein is reputed to have said, "The problems that exist in the world today cannot be solved by the level of thinking that created them."

You will never bring change to your church by continuing to lead in the same way you led before. We would like to present five major shifts in the way we think about leadership that must take place if we are to see the body of Christ emerge healthy, organically, and become fruitful in this world. These shifts are meant to get you off of the merry-go-round and back into the grassroots influence of the kingdom of God that you have always hoped for.

LEADERSHIFT: FROM COSMOS TO KINGDOM

For years the Christian church has looked to the world for effective leadership methods and structures. The result has been a church that more closely resembles a business than a family. It's time that church leaders measured their current ways of thinking against the Holy Scriptures.

Christ's disciples were steeped in the leadership ideals of their generation as well. They had visions of fame and power and wanted to secure their position in what they saw as a coming hierarchy, as demonstrated by the story of James and John in Chapter Seven. The world around them operated in such a way as to exalt some and put down others. Power was based on position, with those on top wielding it over those beneath them. Sound familiar? The world hasn't changed much.

This system of order is an ever-present reality. The Bible calls it the *cosmos,* the system by which the world operates. All of us have been immersed in it and often find it difficult to imagine an alternative. The problem we have is that this system came into being through the fall of humankind, is dominated and operated by Satan, and by its very nature is opposed to the rule of God. When we look to this system for answers to the hows and whys of leading the people of God, we discover methods and mind-sets that will never yield the results we hope for.

When Jesus began His public ministry, He came preaching the kingdom of God. He made statements like "the kingdom of

God is in your midst" and "the kingdom of heaven is at hand."
He taught His disciples to pray, "Thy kingdom come, Thy will be
done on earth as it is in heaven." We believe that there is one day
coming a literal, physical kingdom in which Jesus will rule as king.
We also believe that God's kingdom exists now wherever and
whenever an individual or group submits to His will. The kingdom
of God implies the rule of God. When we pray, "Thy kingdom come, Thy will be done," we are first and foremost asking
that our hearts, minds, and actions be submitted to the will of
God in Christ Jesus. Whenever a believer submits to God, the
kingdom of God is present.

So now in the world there are two opposing systems, the
cosmos and the kingdom. For the church to be what it is meant
to be in Christ, it must operate on the principles of the kingdom
and not the cosmos.

Jesus said to His disciples, "You know that the rulers of the
Gentiles lord it over them and their great men exercise authority
over them. It is not so among you" (Matt. 20:25). This phrase "not
so among you" should be ringing loudly in our ears. He is telling
His disciples in no uncertain terms that leadership in His kingdom
is not about the top-down exercise of authority or control. Let
me say that again. Leadership is not about top-down command
or control.

In the kingdom we are simply to connect people to Christ's
authority and rulership, not submit them to our own. There is no
chain of command in the kingdom—that is a cosmos idea. Authority is not delegated downward in the kingdom; it is distributed
outward. Each person is connected to Christ who holds all the
authority, and each person is to connect others to that same Lord
(authority). There is equal access, equal empowerment, and equal
status in the kingdom.

Our focus is simple: all that is required for a church to be
transfused is a rock-solid trust in the presence of Jesus and the
DNA He provides. As leaders, we have a tendency to hear this and
instantly think we're already doing it. It is because of this that we
continue to examine common church practices and leadership
mind-sets and expose them as wholly inadequate to the true
nature of the church. You simply cannot function with a cosmos
mindset and the kingdom mindset at the same time. You can only

have one master. You are either promoting a cosmos chain of command or you are empowering people in the kingdom; there is no middle ground on this.

LEADERSHIFT: FROM MANAGEMENT TO ENGAGEMENT

Management implies the efficient use and exploitation of available resources to accomplish a task or goal. If the church is organized in such a way that its primary focus is on the accomplishment of tasks and goals, it becomes an organization that needs to be managed. Most businesses are operated this way because they are organized around the purpose of making a profit. Good managers work hard to order and use resources in the most effective way. This minimizes waste and maximizes productivity. We must draw a distinction, however, between the type of leadership necessary in an organization and that needed in a living organism.[1]

A body is organized quite differently than a business. Each part is designed to work in concert with the rest so that health and growth are achieved for the whole. Each part is directed by the head to accomplish its work in the most effective way possible.

The functions of a healthy human body are directed by the brain. Some are directed consciously and some are directed unconsciously, but all are directed by the brain. The brain emits a signal that is carried by the spinal cord and an immense network of nerves to the particular organ it wishes to communicate with. That organ then responds by obeying the command it has received. There is effectively no organ between the brain and the rest of the body.

Most churches are structured in a way that marginalizes the communication between the Head of the church and His body. Instead of asking, "What can I do for God?" we should learn to ask, "What does God want to do through me?" And this question should be asked not by church leaders alone but by every believer on the planet.

We must teach all believers to engage the Head and to seek direction from Jesus and His Spirit. If we can shift our focus from results to health, we will find that we will have them both.

The focus of church leadership must be a healthy body with healthy DNA. If we put our time and effort toward helping individual believers learn to listen and respond to Jesus and His Spirit, we will find that He can and will lead them to fruitfulness.

In 1 Corinthians 2, we are told, "Who among men knows the thoughts of a man except the spirit of the man, which is in him? Even so the thoughts of God no one knows except the Spirit of God. Now we have received, not the spirit of the world, but the Spirit who is from God, that we might know the things freely given to us by God."

A spiritual leader in Christ's church is more concerned with the success of the people they are engaged with than they are in the overall success of the leader's vision and plan. This is a sacrifice, but it will mean a better church in the end, much better. A leader in such an environment must learn to be comfortable without a few things:

1. Constant clarity of direction.
2. A plan that is measurable and unchangeable.
3. Control over outcomes.
4. Measurable success.
5. Security in institutional resources.

While we see that shepherding a flock may involve both leadership and management, when church is viewed more like a business enterprise, management is likely a problem. It is essential that a leader engage the people in such a way that they are hearing the voice of the Shepherd and are able to follow Him in faith into whatever direction He desires. This may take people outside of the walls of the institution and into mission beyond the scope of an organization. A manager may have trouble with this "waste of resource." This is not as much a management skill as it is engagement . . . with the Lord, with His people, and with His mission (DNA).

One of the most essential leadership practices in an organic church is what we call "intentional neglect." When a particular ministry no longer has the same person carrying its weight, we counsel leaders to not prop it up by assigning new people to its post. Instead we suggest that you intentionally neglect it and watch and see what God does. Let God move in people and move people in. If He wants that program to continue He will put it in the heart of someone to lead, if not, let it die so something new can be born. Intentional neglect requires faith that the Head has a plan and then submits to that plan believing that Jesus knows what He is doing and it will be better than any plan the pastoral staff can come up with. This is something a manager would not naturally be inclined to do. When we begin to recognize that development of people is more important than managing systems and programs, then we will often be led to sacrifice a program for the benefit of people.

Following are five contrasts between the mentality of a manager and that of a leader who is engaged:

1. A manager focuses on what is, while a leader focuses on what can be.
2. You can manage resources, but leadership is only about people.
3. A manager maintains the status quo, while a leader challenges it.
4. A manager is often risk-averse, while a leader sees risk as a positive engagement.
5. A manager is concerned with doing things right, while a leader is concerned with doing the right things.

It is God's intention that His children be guided by His Spirit. Just as the human body is animated by the human spirit, the body of Christ must be animated by the Spirit of God. To settle for anything less is to settle for a cheap imitation of the spiritual reality intended for each of us.

LEADERSHIFT: FROM POSITION TO SUBMISSION

"Their great men exercise authority over them. It's not that way among you. The greatest among you shall be the servant of all"

(Matt. 20:25, 26). With these words Jesus forever changed the paradigm of leadership in the body of Christ, or at least it should be so.

If authority is not to be understood as the right to control others, what is it? It is the right to build up those who are willing to follow in ways that will enable them to become all God wants them to be so that they may accomplish all that He wants them to accomplish in the time they have on this earth. Speaking of his God-given authority for the church in Corinth, Paul says that such authority was given to build them up and not to tear them down (2 Cor. 10:8).

Jesus made it clear that "all authority in heaven and earth" belongs to Him. This means that no legitimate authority exists outside of Christ. That is a thought with profound implications. If Christian leaders use their position to influence others to do things that are not ordered by Jesus Himself, the source of their authority is illegitimate. In a very real sense, a leader who does not understand submission will never truly understand authority. All true authority begins with submission to the one True Authority. If you do not know how to submit, then you do not know how to lead. This is because all the authority is with Christ, not in any position or chain of command. In the church, the extent to which you are in submission is the extent you have access to the authority of Christ.

The truth is that when Christ died and rose again to secure our forgiveness and provide us with eternal life, He also set us free to live no longer for our own will but for the will of God. As Rick Warren says in the opening line of *The Purpose-Driven Life*, "It's not all about you."[2] We believe that this message is obscured when the extremes we go to in order to attract listeners scream, "It's all about you." Because of this, many, Christians are lulled into the habit of participating only in those Christian activities that are comfortable or enjoyable for them. They willingly acquiesce to the idea that their part in the expansion of the kingdom of God is to attend the church's programs and give financially to support them. All this serves to further the misconception that the people in authority do the work and everyone else is there to provide support. We believe that every believer has a special role to play in the furtherance of God's rule on this planet. If the majority of them are lulled into believing that their role is minimal, the whole of the body of Christ will suffer for it. Every believer needs to be taught to follow Jesus and then be released to do exactly that.

The believers in Christ, indwelt by the Spirit of Christ, are the most powerful beings on the planet, yet Christian leaders continually underestimate this reality and settle for churches in which these glorious beings remain stabled. They must be built up to understand their place in the cosmos and the kingdom. A leader who understands that he or she has been given the authority to do just that will do well.

Because humans are created as free moral agents, following Jesus is a choice. So even though Christ has been given "all authority in heaven and earth," not all people follow. God could insist, but He doesn't. This should tell us something. If Almighty God allows His creatures to resist His will, who are we to do otherwise? Christ has given us an example to follow. He chooses to woo His followers into obedience. He provides them with everything they need through His never-ending grace. As leaders, we must do everything in our power to help all believers reach their full potential as children of God.

I (Neil) remember having a conversation with my mentor Carol Davis about some calendar dates. Twice in the conversation my CMA leadership meetings interfered with what we were trying to plan. Carol asked me how often our leadership board met and I said, "Every month." She paused, looked back at me with sad eyes and said, "Oh you poor thing." I responded, "No, it's not like that, not at all! We like meeting; our times together are usually the highlight of our month." In fact, at that time two of our team flew to LA for the meetings every month at their own expense! Imagine having meetings that people will pay to be a part of! We have learned in Church Multiplication Associates to meet regularly without an agenda or a leader. We actually believe that the Head of the church has an agenda that we can discover if we listen. It has become our practice to meet and pray and wait until the Lord gives us direction. When the Lord does give direction, all of us are in agreement about what that direction is because we discovered it together. Our leadership team comes together in submission, not strategy. This will not work well if the people in the room all come with self-interest that dominates their own thoughts. The people in such a meeting need to lay aside their own agenda, reputation, and ambition and practice mutual sub-mission under the Head who has all the authority. When that happens you may have a meeting that will blow you away. Typically, a business meeting with a stacked agenda does not accomplish as much.

Why not schedule a retreat, alone or with other leaders, to seek the Lord's direction? Spend time in prayer, and don't be afraid of silence. Listen for the still, small voice of God, and begin to make the changes He asks for. Every journey begins with a first step. As to the church, constantly remind people of who they are in Christ. Encourage them to pray for guidance and listen for answers. Teach them to trust the direction they receive and take their own steps in obedience to their master. Jesus is, in fact, the Head of His body, the church. Let's lay aside our own position, acknowledge His, and let Him lead.

LEADERSHIFT: FROM CONTROL TO ORDER

In Chapter Four, Phil told you of the response his elders initially had to these concepts: "Nothing will ever get done." This is a common objection to moving from a highly controlled and managed environment to one that encourages freedom and spon-taneity. So how do things get done? Believe it or not, people can and will do far more than you can imagine. The secret is in moving from control to order.

For many church leaders, control and order are synonymous. It is hard to even conceive of order in the church without control. As we train people all over the world, it is common for people to express the fear that if they stop controlling things, chaos will ensue, and all sorts of unhealthy things will take over the church. Heresy will break out. Immorality will consume lives. All spiritual growth will be stunted. But are these fears legitimate? We believe that order and control are two very different things and that control does not necessarily lead to order and order is not depen-dent on human control.

We've already seen that Christ has rejected the command-and-control model of leadership common in the world for one in which leaders take responsibility for serving others by encouraging and releasing them to their full potential. At first this seems impractical. But on closer examination its genius is revealed. Control has a way of hindering innovation and stifling full and complete effort. People will often do what's asked of them and nothing more. In a church environment where believers are asked only to fulfill roles that further the particular goals and aspirations of that church or that church's leadership, they often miss seeing other opportunities God might put in their paths as legitimate and therefore fail to act on them.

Dee Hock, founder and CEO emeritus of VISA USA and VISA International, addresses similar organizational issues in an article titled "The Chaordic Organization: Out of Control and into Order."[3] Concerning management techniques common to business and the church, he opines, "The most abundant, least expensive, most under utilized and frequently abused resource in the world is human ingenuity; the source of that abuse is archaic, Industrial Age institutions and the management practices they spawned." We would take it a step past human ingenuity to the genius of the presence of Christ. Hock blames the mind-set of the Industrial Revolution for spawning management practices that seek to control others to produce predetermined uniform outcomes, but we believe it is the sinful human nature within us that desires to control outcomes. Because these approaches make sense to our fallen minds, we must double our efforts to fight against them.

For Hock, the truest and most virulent form of organization is the one that removes artificial controls and relies instead on characteristics common to human nature to bring about order. Capitalism is a similar theory. It relies on human self-interest and the forces of a common marketplace to create an atmosphere where people are free to pursue their personal interests in a way that benefits them and others. This still caters to a fallen human nature.

But for the believer there is something more. We are individually and corporately indwelt by the Spirit of God and the person of Jesus. The believer who freely follows Jesus is not just acting out of self-interest but is able to act out of love. A disciple of Christ is not "out of control" but is being controlled by the living God (2 Cor. 5:13–15).

If you think about the way a human body is organized, you will recognize that each part does what is necessary to fulfill its particular role without knowledge or care for what the other parts are doing. As each part fulfills its role, all the other parts benefit, and the whole body becomes healthy and productive. Imagine trying to manage every function or process that takes place in the human body. Not even the most powerful computer in the world could accomplish that task.

If we are going to see the body of Christ healthy and flourishing, we will need to learn to trust Christ's ability to actually control His own body. Larry Richards calls this "radical supernaturalism."[4] We're not sure it's really radical at all. It may seem radical, but think about it. We serve a God who has promised to be with us always and to use us to do good works that He Himself has prepared. It seems to us that not to believe this is radical. Answer this simple question: Is the God who created and sustains the universe capable of *actually* leading and empowering His people? If you can answer in the affirmative, you have taken a step toward organic living.

There are two things that should quell our fears that things will get out of control. The first is the presence of Jesus in the life of each believer, and the second is the DNA His presence produces. If a person is listening and willing to obey, Jesus will lead that believer into fruitfulness just as He has promised. As we stated earlier, Jesus established the DNA of the believer and His body, the church, when He said, "I am with you always," "Love one another," and "Make disciples." His presence produces a life that reflects and embodies these three things and will produce not only order but also effectiveness beyond our wildest imaginations. Just as your body relies on your internal DNA to orchestrate the growth and outcomes of each part of your body, the DNA of Christ's kingdom will do the same to His Body. Trust it more than you do your own ability.

Some will ask, "But what if people do not listen correctly or choose to do the wrong things . . . or even to do the right things in the wrong way?" Yes, we run that risk in an organic living system, don't we? But the truth is we still run the same risk in an organizational system that runs on a top-down chain of command and control model of leadership. The real question is, "Do you trust in your own ability to control people more than Christ's ability to lead them?" There will be abuses either way because we are in a fallen world with an enemy seeking to steal, kill, and destroy all that is good. We suggest that an organic approach can bring freedom, life, and fruit while a command and control approach will not.

LEADERSHIFT: FROM SELF-INTEREST TO SELFLESSNESS

We believe that God has created each of us for greatness—not necessarily a greatness that can be seen with the naked eye, but one that is visible to the God who sees all things. We have, over the past several years, witnessed a phenomenon in the Christian world, the rise of the "celebrity pastor." In his article "The Evangelical Industrial Complex and the Rise of Celebrity Pastors," Skye Jethani argues that the "market-driven cycle of megachurches, conferences, and publishers results in an echo chamber where the same voices, espousing the same values, create an atmosphere where ministry success becomes equated with audience aggregation."[5] As pastors gain more celebrity, it is not uncommon for them to become more and more isolated from their congregations. We know of many churches where it is almost impossible for a church member to have a conversation, let alone a relationship, with the pastor. As Bob Hyatt blogged, "It should not be easier for CNN to get in touch with a pastor than people in his/her own congregation."[6]

It is our contention that this same sort of process often takes place on a smaller scale between the pastor of a small to medium-sized church and his congregation. Because we are created for greatness, there is something inside us that seeks affirmation of that greatness in the wrong place—the eyes of other humans instead of the eyes of God. Like those pastors whose celebrity is more widespread, we must all check ourselves to see that our actions are not motivated by a desire for notoriety, influence, or some other sort of personal prestige. We can feed these desires when we position ourselves in the church in ways that make us indispensible. Sometimes we're looking for notoriety, influence, or prestige in the eyes of God by trying to produce something that will make Him proud. On the surface this seems logical, but it causes our own performance and ego to get caught up with the church in an unhealthy way.

One of the keys to leading your church to greater fruitfulness is to set your own agenda aside. Make it less about what you want to see happen and more about what you see God doing in and through others. In this way your agenda moves from being about reaching some predetermined goal to being more about releasing others to follow the path to fruitfulness God has ordained for them.

We have already said much about Jesus' admonition that "whoever wishes to become great among you shall be your servant" (Matt. 20:26). Servant leadership is a description we all hope to reflect, but we don't often take time to consider what it really means. Jesus is talking about our becoming slaves of others. Does this mean that we should put ourselves in a position to be dominated by those we are supposed to lead? We don't think so. But it certainly doesn't mean we should expect others to serve us or our agendas. To be a servant leader, we must put the best interests of those we serve ahead of our own. We must seek to draw out their giftedness and help them reach their full potential. This requires supernatural wisdom and a firm belief that God is able and willing to work in the hearts and lives of His people. Servant leaders will find themselves pleading with God to fill the hearts and minds of His followers with love, patience, kindness, and wisdom. Servant leaders will listen to the dreams and aspirations of those they lead and help them take steps toward realizing those goals.

One of the biggest hurdles for the servant leader to clear is the reluctance of Christians to believe that it's possible for them to live as fruitful servants of God. Ephesians 4:11–12 says, "And He gave some *as* apostles, and some *as* prophets, and some *as* evangelists, and some *as* pastors and teachers, for the equipping of the saints for the work of service, to the building up of the body of Christ." Notice that the word *work* is singular. We think this hints at the idea that a major step in the process of equipping followers of Christ is helping them come to a place where they are willing to set aside their own will for the will of God. Just as we are saying that leaders need to move from selfishness to selflessness, we believe that every believer who wishes to follow Christ must do the same.

For our churches to thrive, we must promote a culture that is constantly reinforcing these truths and expecting nothing less than full surrender to the cause of Christ. As you and those you lead begin to act on these truths you will find that God will meet you in very personal and intimate ways and that the transformation Paul spoke of will become a reality in your experience.

Leadership in the kingdom is very different than in the cosmos, and we have articulated several shifts that must take place to release a kingdom culture in the church. In Chapter Nine we will address the most basic role that every person in the church is called to fulfill.

CHAPTER NINE

DISCIPLES, DISCIPLES, DISCIPLES

In real estate, the most important factors are: location, location, location. In church the most important missional objectives are: disciples, disciples, disciples. You can have the best programs, rocking music, state of the art facilities, and uplifting messages, but if your disciples are weak and unengaged with Christ then your church is weak. Your church is only as good as its disciples.

As we have emphasized throughout this book, the task of a leader in a transfusional church is really quite simple. In fact, the true missional objective for virtually every person in Christ's body is: *listen to Jesus and do what He says.* If we all just did that, everything would turn out great!

We believe that the Great Commission is about making disciples. We also believe that much of what has been passed off as discipleship has woefully missed the mark. As the church has become more and more institutionalized, it has required more and more effort to sustain its programs. Pastors and church leaders spend a great deal of time looking for people to fill a variety of jobs that keep the church running. Being a disciple is much more than being a cog that keeps the wheels of the institution turning.

It's not about watching kids in the nursery, singing in the choir, handing out bulletins, counting the offering, or directing parking in the parking lot. None of these things are bad, and you will likely be blessed by doing them, but not if they are done at the expense of truly being Christ's disciple. Jesus died for more than a good Sunday service. He died to set people free from sin and death and to transform their lives from uselessness to usefulness.

Remember, "We are His workmanship, created in Christ Jesus for good works which He prepared beforehand for us to do" (Eph. 2:10). When believers are relegated to doing simple tasks in support of an institution, they are robbed of the opportunity to be what they were meant to be. They become convinced that they are doing something worthwhile (and they generally are), but they often assume that that's all that's required or expected.

It has become commonplace to hear believers refer to themselves as Christ followers. This is a step in the right direction, but what does it actually entail? To be a Christ follower, one must follow Christ. Seems simple enough doesn't it?

Many understand following Jesus to be synonymous with knowing His Word. In many churches the one who knows the most about theology is considered the best disciple. It is often assumed that the more theology you have mastered, the more mature you are, even if it is simply knowledge void of practice. We believe that knowledge of the Scriptures is a necessary ingredient in the discipleship process, but to equate knowledge with discipleship is a huge mistake. When we do this, we forget that Jesus did not command us to teach them "all He has commanded" us but to teach them to "*obey* all that He has commanded" us. Any form of discipleship that doesn't focus on helping others live out their faith in real terms is not discipleship at all. Even those who seem to understand this truth sometimes fall into the trap of acquiring the requisite obedience by using outside pressure. This too results in an anemic follower of Jesus.

The temptation is to teach people to look to the Scriptures for instructions on how to live a good life. We believe that the Bible is the truth, the inerrant and infallible Word of God, but when people search the Scriptures for rules to live by, they settle for a life that is less than it is meant to be.

It's clear from the gospel accounts that Jesus lived His life for the will of His Father. You'll find Him saying such things as "The Son of Man can do nothing of Himself unless it is something

He sees the Father doing" (John 5:19) and "I did not speak on My own initiative, but the Father Himself who sent Me has given Me a commandment as to what to say and what to speak. I know that His commandment is eternal life, therefore the things I speak, I speak just as the Father has told Me" (John 12:49). And again, "I have come down from heaven not to do My own will but the will of Him who sent Me" (John 6:38). Jesus lived His life in constant connection with His Father. "I and the Father are one" (John 10:30). He was perpetually obedient, even to the point of death on a cross. Jesus came to fulfill a specific mission: "to give His life a ransom for many" (Mark 10:45b). How is it that we seem to think that a life of generic good works in conformity to the written word is all God wants from us?

1 Corinthians 12 further supports this thinking. "Now there are varieties of gifts, but the same Spirit. And there are varieties of ministries, and the same Lord. There are varieties of effects, but the same God who works all things in all persons. And each one is given the manifestation of the Spirit for the common good." Isn't it obvious that this infinite variety of gifts, ministries, and results is indicative of an infinite variety of works God intends to accomplish through His children? How is this to happen when leaders take it upon themselves to prescribe the work to be done by each individual and each individual is happy to let them? Jesus is the Head of His body, and He must be allowed to direct each member as He sees fit.

The Scriptures have much to say about God and life, and when the principles it contains are observed and practiced, they can be of infinite value. But to substitute a relationship with the Bible for a relationship with Jesus is a fatal mistake. Paul makes it clear in his letter to the churches of Galatia that to live by an outside standard or set of rules is to seek a gospel other than the grace of Christ. Jesus, in a comment to the religious leaders of His day, agrees: "You search the Scriptures because you think that in them you have eternal life, but it's these that testify about Me" (John 5:39). The Scriptures are meant to bring us to Jesus so that He can write His words on our hearts.

We believe that the essence of discipleship is a vital personal relationship with Christ. This personal ongoing encounter with the Creator is the cornerstone of what it means to be a Christ follower.

Imagine that you lived next door to Kobe Bryant. (We're both Laker fans, so this illustration works for us. Any notable person of interest will do.) As you watch out your window, you see him coming and going. You know what kind of car he drives, what sort of clothes he wears, what his schedule is like, and other little details about his life. You might even overhear conversations between him and his wife, his children, and others he might know. You would probably make sure all of your friends knew about your special connection to Kobe, wouldn't you? You'd tell them all the little secrets you know (especially if you heard him and his wife fighting) and remind them that, after all, you do live next door. In this scenario you know a lot of things about Kobe Bryant, but you don't really know Kobe. To get to know him, you would have to engage him. You'd have to go out your door and talk directly to him. And once wouldn't be good enough. You'd have to spend some time with him. Maybe talking over the fence or in the driveway or inviting him over for dinner. The more time you spent with him, the more you would get to know him. You'd discover his likes and dislikes, his personality quirks, and maybe even his dreams and aspirations. One thing is for sure: none of this is possible if you never get out of your house and engage him in a personal way.

We believe that many Christians find themselves in a similar position. They listen to stories about Jesus on the radio or in sermons. They might read the Bible and therefore see Him from a somewhat closer vantage point, but unfortunately, this is as close as they ever get. Seeing Christ in the Scriptures is not good enough.

Believers must be challenged to engage the living Jesus in an intimate personal way every day. We are only truly followers of Jesus when we look to Him for direction and do what He tells us.

Some will say that Jesus has spoken to us in His Word and that's all we need. In contrast to just hearing the Scriptures, God states that, "in these last days, He has spoken to us in His Son" (Heb. 1:2). And "This is my beloved Son, listen to Him" (Mark 9:7). And "My sheep, hear My voice and follow Me" (John 10:27).

We could go on. Christ's promises to dwell with us, always be with us, and never leave or forsake us are further testament to the intimacy necessary if we are to experience His power and presence in the accomplishment of the mission He has given us.

Think about it. Has He commissioned us to make disciples of all the nations and then left us to our own devices to accomplish the task? Absolutely not! As Paul says again, "It is no longer I who live but Christ lives in me" (Gal. 2:20). If we are to make disciples, true followers of Jesus, then we must help them, first and always, connect with Him. He must become their teacher, and they must become His student. They must learn to hear His voice and follow Him and Him alone.

Getting those who have become used to depending on human leadership for direction to transfer that allegiance to Christ is a tall order. Once people are set in their patterns, it's difficult for them to change. Don't, however, fall into the trap of believing that it's impossible. What is impossible for humans is in no way impossible for God. Our whole thesis comes down to the belief that the Almighty God is present and at work in His children. Miguel Labrador of Missional Outreach Network has said, "We don't establish the DNA of a disciple in the making of disciples. If indeed they are a disciple of Christ, He already did that. We help them to unveil, understand, and unleash their genetic potential."[1] God has a vested interest in seeing His children fully matured and doing His bidding in this world.

We believe that if we help each and every believer see this truth, it will have a profound impact on the church and the world. After all, it's His command through the pen of Paul:

> I urge you, brethren, by the mercies of God, to present your bodies a living and holy sacrifice, acceptable to God, which is your spiritual service of worship. And do not be conformed to this world, but be transformed by the renewing of your mind, so that you may prove what the will of God is, that which is good and acceptable and perfect. [Rom. 12:1–2]

The choice to surrender to the will of God is a choice every believer must make. It is the task of leadership to clear the way so that decision can and will be made. May the Lord, Himself, bring every believer to yield his or her heart completely to Him and to His good, acceptable, and perfect will. Amen.

There are many ways to encourage this process to take place. We have discovered one approach that works very well and reproduces very easily. If you are familiar with Neil's writing, you are most likely familiar with Life Transformation Groups. LTGs, as we call them, are the backbone of much of what we do to make and release disciples. Because LTGs have received so much previous exposure, we won't treat them exhaustively here, but we will provide you with a brief overview. If you want to learn more, you can find more information at http://cmaresources.org or by reading Neil's books, *Cultivating a Life for God* or *Search and Rescue*.[2]

LTGs are groups of two or three people of the same sex who meet weekly for mutual accountability. The meetings take about an hour and focus on three areas: Bible reading (*divine truth*), confession of sin (*nurturing relationships*), and prayer for lost people (*apostolic mission*). During the week the group will read a previously agreed passage of Scripture. We suggest at least twenty to thirty chapters. When they meet, they will ask each other if they did the reading. If not, they will read the same passage again. We understand that twenty to thirty chapters might seem like a lot, but we actually want it to be difficult enough that they won't finish every week. When one or more persons don't finish the reading, they read it again. This is desirable because it builds in the world's best teacher, repetition. It's hard to get people to accept this at first, but soon they see the wisdom in it. The second thing they do together is confess their sins. We have designed a variety of cards with different types of accountability questions on them. The disciples ask each other the questions and answer them honestly. The intimacy and sense of accountability this provides cannot be overstated. The third thing they do when they meet is establish a list of unbelievers to pray for. Each person provides two or three people for the list. They write these names on the card and pray a number of prayers asking God for their souls every time they read the Bible (or more often if they want). These groups don't need leaders. All they need are people willing to work the process. When they do, we find that they become internally motivated to follow Jesus and be used by Him in this world. They become disciples making disciples. And perhaps the most important quality of LTGs is that they plant the DNA of a healthy church within the smallest unit of church life: two or three people. When the DNA is in the disciples, it is in the church.

You may have another way to get the job done. Great! But if you don't, this strategy has proved its worth throughout the world. Give it a try and see what happens.

Making disciples starts slow and small, but with the right mind-set, you can initiate a church transfusion, one life at a time. In Chapter Ten we will share with you a rather simple and organic plan to bring that transfusion about. The bottom line, though, is always the same for you and for all whom you influence: *listen to God and do what He says.*

CHAPTER TEN

WATER THE GREEN SPOT

In 1943, at the height of World War II, the engineers coming from the same schools being taught by the same professors were not producing the technological breakthroughs that were needed. To get faster and better results, Lockheed decided to try something different. The company selected its most creative engineers and put them all in a tent set up at the end of a runway next to a plastics factory in Burbank, California. The engineers were told to think together outside the box on a specific project.

The members of this group began to push boundaries and try new things. Without all the red tape of the standard business bureaucracy, they were able to get things done much faster, usually ahead of schedule, and often with nothing more than a verbal agreement and a handshake.

They became known as "skunk works" because of the smell of the plastic factory wafting into the tent. The name came from the *Li'l Abner* comic strip, and it stuck. Today *skunk works* has become a technical term in research and development and in the diffusion of innovation. It is widely used in business, engineering, and technical fields to describe a group within an organization given a high degree of autonomy and unhampered by bureaucracy, often tasked with working on advanced or secret projects. The original Lockheed skunk works (which still exists) is responsible for some of the most notable advancements in technology in aerospace and defense. Such things as stealth technology and smart bombs were developed there. The Macintosh computer was developed in a skunk works project under the demanding leadership of Steve Jobs and Steve Wozniak. The first laptop was designed and developed by a skunk works group that was literally kept secret from the very organization that made it and had determined that it was not a worthy investment—Toshiba.

The truth is that the church in the United States has needed skunk works for some time. For many decades all our leaders were coming from the same education system and bringing the same paradigm to the church. By God's grace, however, many have emerged recently that are injecting the kingdom with new ideas and fresh expressions of church free from the old institutional systems that tend to perpetuate the same old stuff while stuck in a constant mode of self-preservation.

When you lead a church that is established, you may need a skunk works operation of your own if you want to experience a transfusion of organic life and principles into it. We have found that a systemwide corporate change launched all at once from the top down tends to diffuse any real impact and does little to actually transform a church or its people. Such a scenario may bring about programmatic change, but it will not be internal, grassroots, and organic. That is why we suggest you launch a skunk works project on the side. It will allow the change to come from the people rather than the pastoral staff alone. You are far more likely to get buy-in on a smaller scale at first and then see sustained progress as more and more people adopt the new ideas.

As a leader of your church, you can always cast vision for change, but the actual implementation may require a slower and smaller start if it is to yield holistic transformative results. Any true organic change must be internal, relational, and advance virally—like a contagion from one person to the next. We believe that this requires that you start small with a unique group and let its influence spread. A skunk works approach is the best way to initiate this sort of transformation.

SKUNK WORKS CONSIDERATIONS

When you initiate a skunk works project, a few things are important to consider.

SELECT YOUR INNOVATORS CAREFULLY

It is not necessary to involve many people in the beginning. It is far more important to select the right people. Every successful skunk works story emphasizes one common characteristic: the people were hand-selected, and the criteria for that selection were very important. You want people who are creative risk takers willing to try something new. Select people who will look at a situation and see opportunity rather than obstacles. You want people who tend to ask, "Why not?" when presented with an idealistic solution to a challenging problem. It is OK to combine thinkers with doers, but to start with only thinkers will be lethal to the project and to start with only doers will be hit or miss.

There is no reason that you can't have more than one skunk works project at a time, but we suggest you not spread the few innovative people you have over too many projects. If the senior leader tends to be a more innovative risk taker, that person can certainly be part of the initial experimentation, but this is not necessary for success. What is necessary is that the leader be supportive of the change and be willing to place the overall good of the church over his or her own ego.

Most senior leaders tend to think of themselves as innovative, even when they are not, so seek objective advice and be willing to stay out of the way. The truth is that if this is going to work, your initial innovators will likely let you know who they are and will either not be stopped or will go somewhere else to get it done, so simply listen well to what more creative people are passionate about and give them permission to proceed.

GRANT PERMISSION

These initial individuals should know that they have permission to try new things and even to fail. Every creative endeavor requires many iterations. These people need to know that they will not have the rug pulled out from under them after the first failed attempt.

Often younger people will be most drawn to this type of endeavor. Young people are naturally more idealistic and also have more freedom to try new things. The young do not have as many entrenched viewpoints and are more open to new ideas. Unfortunately, they may not have the experience to know that things will not work perfectly the first time. You may need to tell them that it is OK to fail in their attempt to do something great. The late Ralph Winter, founder of the U.S. Center for World Mission, often said, "Risks are not to be evaluated in terms of the probability of success but in terms of the value of the goal."[1] That is an insight worth repeating to others.

We suggest that you consider allowing the new skunk works project to progress for a time under the radar at the church. We are not condoning the keeping of secrets so much as not making a big splash that sets unreal expectations on a small band trying out something new and radical. Let the skunk workers flounder a bit and make mistakes without the pressure of all eyes being on their efforts if you can.

SET BOUNDARIES IF YOU MUST—BUT NOT MANY

After giving them permission, you may want to set whatever boundaries are needed. There are almost always boundaries of some sort when you talk about established churches. This is one of the prime reasons that starting from scratch is easier than revitalizing what already exists.

Boundaries in established churches are often the very thing that prevents movements from happening. The extent to which you can relieve the skunk works project of boundaries will be the extent to which the new work can thrive. Does that risk problems with the new work? Of course it does, but risk is actually part of the exercise of faith, so that is not bad at all. In fact, often the old culture that you want to revitalize will put a premium on remaining safe, and risk is the prescription for overcoming this lack of faith.

The truth is that a spontaneous multiplication movement will seem out of control, and the more control you demand, the less likely you will be to release any movement. Nevertheless, you likely have some boundaries that must be addressed if you are starting with an already established church or denomination. Always try to remember that the Holy Spirit is more than able to lead those He desires to use.

Some typical boundaries would have to do with how the new work group communicates its new ideas to others, whom they are allowed or encouraged to recruit and not recruit, how the group relates to the church or the denomination, and what financial limitations it has. Is it necessary that the people in the skunk works project attend the Sunday morning worship service? If so, must they come every week? Do they need to tithe or give offerings to the main body? If so, what percentage? Can some of the offerings they receive go toward the new work exclusively? Are they required to practice the ordinances the same as the mother church? Can they baptize their own converts, or must the senior pastor or a paid staff member do all the baptizing? Each of these questions establishes a boundary; in fact, some of them establish entire systems of boundaries. The more restrictive the boundaries, the less likely they will be able to spin off organic reproductive movements.

Ralph Moore, a friend and mentor who is the catalyst behind the Hope Chapels, taught me (Neil) something years ago that I have always valued. Ralph is Foursquare and will likely still be ordained in the Foursquare denomination when he dies (and hopefully that will be a long time away). Every church he ever started has been Foursquare, but that is not true for the people he has sent out. He has always let his church planters decide for themselves if they will be Foursquare or not. There are many churches that are part of the Hope Chapel movement but not Foursquare. When I asked him about this, he said that a movement cannot dictate everything to everyone; we must allow each generation to make up its own mind. Control and movements do not mix.

That is why our own movement, though starting with Grace Brethren pastors, never remained exclusively Grace Brethren. Freedom to make decisions is a vital part of faith, and when we make decisions for people, we stymie their faith and stunt their growth. If you want to birth vital reproductive churches, you must grant them the freedom to choose. The more boundaries there are, the less likely the new works will multiply.

Some boundaries have an expiration date, so let the skunk works group know if a certain boundary is only for the initial phase. That way the group members will be a bit more patient

WATER THE GREEN SPOT   141

about how they set out to initiate change. In fact, if you have to set boundaries, consider putting expiration dates on the boundaries with each breakthrough so that the project can gain more and more freedom as it develops and demonstrates health. You may achieve the best of both worlds in the beginning by acknowledging the need for demonstrated faithfulness while moving toward freedom and the unleashing of movement.

We have found that the fewer the boundaries, the better, so long as the people involved are centered on Christ. For instance, if your goal is to have people so sold out to Christ that they will not hesitate to tell their family and friends the gospel, you probably don't have to set a boundary about being gospel-centered.

We strongly suggest that you take a more centered approach than a bounded approach to leadership in this new work. In *The Shaping of Things to Come,* Mike Frost and Alan Hirsch, expanding on the writings of Missiological anthropologist Paul D. Hiebert, elaborate on the differences between a bounded set (putting up fences) and a centered set (digging a well in the Australian outback to keep livestock close).[2]

A bounded-set approach delineates everything from the outset and defines people as "in" or "out" based on how they relate to the boundaries that are established. You probably understand this because most churches and denominations function this way. Doctrinal distinctives of a denomination are a wall in a group's bounded set. Church practices may be a wall in your bounded set: Sunday school curriculum, what school you attended, who administers the communion, or how you baptize may all be walls that define who is in and who is out of your particular culture. Attendance at a weekly service or what day of the week you worship might also be part of your bounded set.

A centered-set approach defines the core values, the convictions that are central and common to all, so strongly that the people are motivated to stay close to each other and to the cause rather than needing to be controlled by any outside boundaries. People are not measured as in or out but rather by their proximity to the centered-set values. In any true multiplication movement, it is essential that the people be governed by a centered-set approach, so it makes sense to start that way with this new skunk works project. For us, the DNA (divine truth, nurturing relationships, and apostolic mission) is our centered-set value system. Hearing the voice of God in the context of loving relationships while on Christ's mission is the glue that holds us together in a centered-set movement. We have resisted all boundaries because we do not want to slow or impede the movement that Christ is birthing—and leading. Taking a centered-set approach will of course mean a different culture for the skunk works project than for the mother church, but that is how change starts.

In John 10, Jesus touches on both forms of governance as he describes the care of sheep both within a "fold" and a "flock." When sheep are in the *fold*, they are in a bounded set. The walls of the fold keep them in line, and the shepherd's work is easier. The sheep are free to venture wherever they want within the walls of the fold; they don't even have to pay much attention. According to John 10, Jesus is the door to get into the fold. Out in the wild of Palestine in the first century, the shepherds would set up simple folds in the open air made of stonewalls with an opening on one side. There was no actual door or gate, but the shepherd would sleep across the doorway.[3]

But the sheep do not stay in the fold, where they would eventually run out of fresh grass and clean water. Jesus leads us outside the walls of the fold and goes on to speak of a *flock*. A flock is bound not by four walls but by its connection to the shepherd. As Jesus says, "My sheep hear My voice and follow Me." We are meant for a whole lot more than staying penned up. We are meant to venture out into the world. It is absolutely essential that we stay close to Jesus and listen to His voice out in the dangerous world where we are lambs surrounded by wolves.

The contrast between a fold and a flock is important to note. In fact, a mistranslation of John 10:16 in the King James Version of the New Testament mixed up the two terms and led to the Roman Catholic Church's doctrine that there is just one true church and everyone needs to be in its fold to be saved. It started with Jerome and the Vulgate, where it says, "Other sheep I have, which are not of this fold: them I must also bring, and they shall hear My voice; and there shall be one *fold*, and one shepherd." The actual translation is that "they shall become one *flock* with one shepherd" (emphasis mine), which is a whole different meaning because it places us outside of the bounded set of a religious system and keeps us all following the voice of our one shepherd wherever He may lead us. Loyalty to Christ is very different from loyalty to the bounded set of a church, and we must always keep this in mind.

The more you can reduce the boundaries, keeping them to an absolute minimum, the better off you will be. The issue is how willing you are to trust Jesus to actually shepherd His flock. In fact, we will go so far as to say that the more boundaries you establish in the beginning, the less likely you will ignite any organic life or movement. Unless your people are free to follow the Great Shepherd out into the world where they live, they will not truly be the church on mission or even true disciples for that matter. The real question is, do you trust the Great Shepherd to lead His flock, or do you trust your own systems and boundaries to manage and control the people? In our opinion, the people of God have been penned up far too long.

That said, it is better to establish some boundaries in the beginning rather than let them be discovered the much harder way—by crossing them and encountering unexpected consequences. Do not take a centered-set approach to your skunk works project only to surprise participants later with a stone wall of fixed boundaries. Many times we have seen young people excited about fulfilling the Great Commission by making disciples only to find that they are in great trouble for having baptized them without permission (as if all authority of heaven and earth is not enough). Be honest. Individuals engaged in the new work will also appreciate not having to waste time and energy pursuing a direction that will ultimately hit a wall.

Start in Places Other Than Your Church Campus

The new project should be born outside the walls of the church building. We have found that if it remains contextually connected to the rest of the church ministries, it will likely carry the same culture. The new transfused work must have apostolic mission within its core being, so what better place is there to begin than out where the people you want to reach are living and working?

In *The Great Good Place*, social commentator Ray Oldenburg coins the term *third place*.[4] Oldenburg defines the first place as your home and the people connected to your home life. He defines your workplace, where we actually spend the most of our time, as the second place. The third place, which he goes on to argue is important in establishing community and civil life together, is the place and people we connect with outside of the other two important places. Robert Putnam in his groundbreaking work *Bowling Alone: The Collapse and Revival of American Community*, argues throughout the book that this third place is essential for our society as a whole.[5] What better place is there for the church to flourish? Recognizing the demise of such places, Starbucks has actually found its niche in providing a third place and made billions of dollars there.

Many consider the church itself to be a third place, and rightly so, but when we exist as our own third place and isolate our lives from others socially, we no longer have influence on the world. We would argue that church should happen wherever life happens. Let this new project be birthed off the church campus in the locale where people live and interact.

Once you start on church grounds, the likelihood of ever getting off campus is weak. But if you start off campus, you will find fewer restrictions in the future and more opportunities in the present. Besides, it is healthy if the church finds itself out in the community figuring out ways to bring the kingdom of God to a place.

Establish Lines of Communication

Make sure that in the very beginning you establish a method of communication so that you are kept aware of how things are

going. Often communication will just be assumed without established channels, and then communication may or may not actually happen, resulting in frustrations on both sides of the project.

We recommend that the senior leadership, no matter how
busy you are, take an interest in the project and be in on the
communication personally. This should probably be more than
just receiving reports. Be in on the meetings and planning as long
as your presence doesn't intimidate the other leaders. When you
are in the meetings, lead with silence. In other words, let other
people speak and share ideas so that they own them, while you
model what it means to empower others. Most church cultures
are designed in such a way that when a senior leader is in the
room, he or she is expected to do most of the talking and have
most of the ideas. If that is the old environment of your church
and you want to transfuse a new DNA into the life of the congregation, this is the place to change the expectations. We have
found that remaining silent, even when it becomes uncomfortable, usually leads to others stepping up.

We strongly suggest that you mentor the new leaders personally. In fact, we have found that the extent that the senior
leadership is vested in the project determines how much the
transfusion can reach the rest of the body. When the senior
leadership is vested in word only, but not in true value, whereas
you have invested time and affection such that you take joy in
the successes and grieve in the difficulties, you are more likely
to spin off a new church than to revitalize an existing one. R&D
is usually about the future, and if the senior leadership is
not leading into the future, the organization has little hope of
getting there.

The balance here is in being a leader who empowers others
and is vested in the project without making them dependent on
you in the process. Our experience is that meeting one-on-one
with the key leaders in a mentoring appointment on a regular
basis (every other week or once a month) is the best solution.
When you meet, listen and ask questions without telling the
apprentice leader what to do. Let these leaders discover for themselves what they need to learn. They will be able to stand on their
own as leaders without being dependent on you, and you will also
model for them how to be an empowering leader for the next
generation. To do this well, you will have to rejoice in another's

success rather than gleaning all the credit yourself. This is hard for some senior leaders who are wired to find success and popularity built on their personality and gifts in the old system, but the old system is broken. If transfusing new life into the church is your aim, you will have to lead differently, which is why we devoted so much space in earlier chapters to leading differently. Neil's book *Organic Leadership: Leading Naturally Right Where You Are* presents principles of mentoring to multiply that can help significantly with this process.

We have found that the leaders who are able to equip and empower others in this manner tend to be surrounded with higher-caliber people because those leaders are trusted by the people—and by the Lord. Leaders who simply use people to get their own results will likely not succeed in the transfusion process and will also find that they are surrounded with lesser-quality leaders. Such leaders will also not multiply because, frankly, God doesn't want any more of them.

There are two benefits to setting up a clear line of communication. First, the people doing the new project will feel valued if you take the time to listen to what they are learning. Second, the people in the church will have more confidence in the project knowing that you are personally connected and the people are not off on their own without any relational accountability.

BLOCK INCOMING HOSTILITIES

As you release a few key people to attempt new practices based on new paradigms of church, it is important that they be protected by the leadership of the church. Using football language, we call this "blocking." The truth is that the enemy of the new is most often the old. Some people may view this new work being started as a threat to a way of life or a church practice that they have long held dear. A kind word and gentle defense from a secure pastor will go a long way to allowing something fresh to occur while keeping peace with everyone else. Let everyone know that this is experimental and needs to be given a chance to develop. Make it your responsibility to intercept any criticism directed against the skunk works project.

Our personal experience is that when someone comes after a person or ministry with a negative complaint, a move toward relationship will often ease much of the hostility. Grant the one with the complaint a listening ear and a positive relational response first. Take time to hear the complaint and validate the one complaining in any way possible before you defend the project. It is often possible to find a legitimate concern to value without necessarily validating the complaint. Often if the one complaining knows that his or her concerns were heard and understood, a lot of problems will be eliminated. There may be times, however, when this is not enough, and you may need to be more assertive in protecting the project.

SHARE REPORTS REGULARLY AND ENTHUSIASTICALLY

In an established congregation, the pulpit is the one place where you can communicate to almost everyone at once. Use this venue to share your own enthusiasm for the new works being done. Tell stories and illustrate your sermons from the new ministry. Give reports of any successes, and ask for prayers from the congregation for this new venture. This is not meant to motivate the unmotivated, for that is useless. But in every congregation there will be others who love Jesus, are frustrated with their current lack of fruitful living, and will be looking for a chance to grow. They need to hear that there is hope and opportunity.

PROVIDE AN AVENUE FOR EARLY ADOPTERS TO JOIN THE SKUNK WORKS

In *Diffusion of Innovation,* Everett M. Rogers identifies five different groups according to the point in the innovative process at which they accept change: (1) innovators, (2) early adopters, (3) early majority, (4) late majority, and (5) laggards.[6] In a typical population, innovators represent only 2.5 percent, early adopters are around 13.5 percent, the early majority weigh in at around 34 percent, and the late majority are about the same. The laggards are around 16 percent of any populace.

Malcom Gladwell, the bestselling author and journalist, took Rogers's ideas and expanded on them to demonstrate that a "tipping point," which will generate a movement and bring change or influence to the whole society, can occur after the early adopters join in.[7] Alan Hirsch and Dave Ferguson, theorizing based on Rogers's and Gladwell's works, say it takes about 16 percent to reach that tipping point.[8]

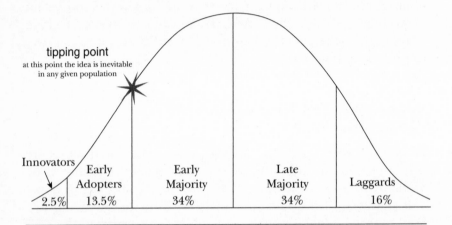

Source: Alan Hirsch and Dave Ferguson, *On the Verge: A Journey into the Apostolic Future of the Church* (Grand Rapids, Mich.: Zondervan, 2011). Used by permission.

This social science provides a clear road map for anyone wanting to bring change to a group of people. Start with innovators, and once you get the early adopters, you will have enough motivation and momentum to eventually change the whole society.

The importance of stringent criteria in the initial selection of a team lessens as early adopters and then an early majority buy in. Don't hear us wrong; it is still important that those who are motivated internally get involved, but it's not necessary that they all be creative risk takers as the work proceeds.

Remember, you are not ending the church your people are accustomed to, at least not initially. You are merely allowing a fresh expression to occur on the side. For transfusion to occur, two different cultures must be present simultaneously. The newer culture should eventually win over the previous one, not in a violent coup but rather in a progression in which health eventually overcomes sickness. We believe that the best sort of change will start gradually and will build momentum over time. A little leavening leavens the whole loaf. A more abrupt and violent transition at the start can create much havoc and may not be necessary. In essence, we are suggesting that you allow some members to pursue a reimagined picture of what life in Christ can be like, let them taste it and tell about it, and over time many others will start to move in that direction. Rather than see this as merely an ending to what your church was before, people can see it as a new direction to a better fulfillment of who you are as a church in the future.

Leverage the new success discovered in the skunk works to lift the whole church. This will be something that likely needs to be done incrementally. John Wooden, former UCLA basketball coach and arguably the most successful coach in all of sports history, once said, "When you improve a little each day, eventually big things occur. . . . Don't look for the quick, big improvement. Seek the small improvement one day at a time. That's the only way it happens—and when it happens, it lasts."

This leveraging of success to the rest of the church is important if your aim is to change the church rather than simply birth a new thing. We actually believe in doing both, but in order to do both, you must allow the health and life found in the more organic skunk works project to filter into the general body of the church. Otherwise you will merely birth new works that are not influencing the body as a whole. There is nothing wrong with birthing new works. We hope that the transfusion of your church will produce many, but here we are talking about how to bring transformation to your existing church.

Every church has a culture, and it's this culture you are seeking to change. When we speak of a tipping point occurring at around 16 percent, we are not suggesting that you seek to recruit that 16 percent to the new way of operating and call it a day. Life change, even for the truest of disciples, is a process. As people in your church continue in relationship with those who are changing, ideas, insights, and experiences will be shared. It's these unscheduled and unscripted moments that ultimately produce change.

Focus on the life and health of the disciples, not the accomplishment of some other goal, whether it be a new church or outreach or anything else. As people learn to follow Jesus, their changed lives will be naturally contagious. Be patient and let Christ work. He will bring about lasting and sometimes unforeseen results. You will be pleasantly surprised.

Most church leaders usually approach change by starting with the elders and leadership staff in hope that the change will work its way down. Phil started this way with Los Altos and saw good results. When I (Neil) began introducing a new way of relating to God, one another, and the world while leading an established church, I intentionally chose not to start with the elders. I didn't make this decision because the elders were bad guys; quite the opposite. I chose to start with the "bad guys," the ones who needed their lives to change. I began with a struggling alcoholic named Kenny. When his life turned around dramatically because of the gospel planted in his soul, people noticed. His life change, and then the subsequent change in the lives of those he influenced, was dramatic. Even the elders started to notice, and a godly jealousy was spurred in them so that some also asked to be part of our new disciple-making project. Godly jealousy can actually be a very useful means of involving people in your transfusion. You can assume that some who are not currently growing have a deep longing inside to be more vital in their faith. Watching other people transformed will call out to that primal desire within them, and they may be spurred to join in the transfusion. Unfortunately, the passage of time and the rut of routine will often lead people into a stale form of faith that needs to be reinvigorated. When people begin to see real change in others, they begin to get excited about what God can do in them. We found that even mature elders have room for life change, but they first had to be hungry for it, and watching a young addict come alive stirred that in them. Kenny eventually became our youth pastor.

Don't expect everyone's full acceptance, and certainly don't wait for it. Don't try to get everyone on board before change begins to be implemented; just build toward a majority. The first 16 percent is enough to change the whole. Learn to work with those motivated few, and don't feel you must include everyone equally. The truth is that every church is made up of people who have different motivations. Expecting full acceptance by all before change can be implemented is a sure death knell for a church.

Even Jesus found that one of his inner band of men was not a true disciple. He instructed us through the parables that the wheat and the tares will grow together. He also told us that it is not until the end that the sheep and the goats are separated. He taught that there are four kinds of soil and three of them receive the message of the kingdom but only one will bear fruit. It is not only unrealistic to expect that every person in an established church is a willing follower of Christ; it is frankly an unbiblical expectation. We believe that one potential mission field in the Western context is in the established churches. Many who attend are Christians but not Christ followers, and there is a big difference. They need to hear the good news that the salvation Jesus offers includes everything they need to live a life of purpose and usefulness to God. Such a life is a grand adventure, and believers need to be encouraged to follow Christ into the wonderful adventure He has for them. This call should be made regularly, but as with evangelizing the lost, not everyone will respond. Keep at it, but don't let the lack of response dissuade you from pressing on.

Many pastors need to be relieved of the responsibility to include every person in the church in everything the church does, especially a skunk works project. This type of mentality has led us to attempt to create churches where everyone can feel comfortable; that's why we have churches full of bad soil that bears no fruit. Trust us, if you allow it, the bad soil will be glad to dictate how you should do church, and the church will not be fruitful. And even if you do make every effort to please these folks, some will still find reason to complain. Stop trying to please everyone; that should never be the goal. The goal is to please the King of Kings; that's it. It is His body, not yours and not anyone else's.

Unfortunately, many pastors take their job description to be to motivate unmotivated people. Every week they spend hours trying to figure out what it will take to get people motivated for one more week and wanting to come back again the next. I (Neil) determined long ago that I would no longer try to motivate unmotivated people, and that set me free. I figure that if the death, burial, and resurrection of Jesus is not enough to motivate them, my sermon probably won't do the job. I no longer feel responsible to chase down people and try to convince them to follow Christ. My life is too short for that.

That said, you do not have to offend people who are not motivated. We are not suggesting that either. What we are suggesting is that you find those who are motivated, release them, and invest there. The rest can keep on doing what they have been doing, whatever that is. We are also suggesting that you no longer let the unmotivated people dictate what church should be about— that is how we end up with consumer-driven churches trying to please the most people possible. Instead of using your sermons to impress and attract Christian consumers, try using them to open their eyes to the truth that Jesus is alive in them and wants to use them to bring good into this world. Many who are seemingly unmotivated are this way because they have never fully understood the implications of the gospel message. We believe that many of these penned-up Christians need to be evangelized not for salvation but with a vision of what salvation truly entails.

In my backyard we have a type of grass called St. Augustine grass. I found out when I became a homeowner that there are many different kinds of grass, and they each have different characteristics. St. Augustine grass is one of the strongest because it grows laterally and spreads rather than simply growing vertically. You have to make sure you want it before you plant it because it is a hardy stock and hard to get rid of once it takes root.

If you look at a lawn with St. Augustine grass that is dead and brown with a single patch of green, don't water the dead stuff; water the green spot and let it spread. That's what we are proposing in this chapter. Let something grow that is alive apart from the bureaucratic institution and politics of normal church, and then pour your life into that.

Usually, if it is organic, it will not cost money. We often say that it doesn't cost a dime to make a disciple; it only costs your life. Pour your life where there is health, and let it multiply and spread so that the life pervades the church body. This is a healthy leadership discipline.

Water the green spot, and let it spread. If it is organic, it will spread all by itself through natural reproduction—of disciples, leaders, and finally groups of spiritual families (or churches). Reproduction is a natural function of all living things. Unfortunately, churches rarely reproduce, which is likely an indication of a health issue. Chapter Eleven addresses this important subject and examines reasons why churches are not reproducing naturally and what it will take to release real health and reproduction.

CHAPTER ELEVEN

HEALTHY REPRODUCTION

The organic church I (Neil) am currently a part of began in 2000 when a drug dealer came to Christ followed by many of his associates and clients. We started meeting in his home. Since then this church has sent off more than fifty church planters to start new works. Many of those daughter churches have planted other churches. I've been able to identify daughter churches as far away as Indiana, Paris, Portland, and San Francisco and granddaughter churches in Arizona, Colorado, Marseille, Chiang Mai, India, and much of Asia. Five years into the experience, I was able to track five networks, five generations of reproduction, five different cities where churches were planted, and more than seventy-five churches started. This has always been a fruitful spiritual family.

The diversity of this church is astonishing. At one point as many as seven different languages were spoken; at another point we had a few senior citizens, three wheelchairs, young singles, married couples, and toddlers. Our worship has included two guitars, congas, bongos, shakers, and a saxophone—but no rehearsals and no music set list, just spontaneous songs of praise. Half of the songs we sing are original songs written by our own people.

I am not sharing this to boast, for if you saw this church, you wouldn't be impressed with it. In the last few years this church has become smaller and in some ways less impressive. These days I sometimes affectionately call us the "island of misfit toys." Usually these days you will find a couple of slightly challenged young men, a bright young man bound to a wheelchair with muscular dystrophy, a single mom with three kids, a recovering drug addict, and one old, overweight church planter. Nevertheless, in the past couple of years this church has planted four churches and sent missionaries to Nicaragua, Massachusetts, and Arizona. Throughout this church's life it has never been larger than twenty people, and today it is usually closer to eight or ten. This is the most reproducing church I have ever been a part of.

Recently someone asked me what I do to get all these people to buy in to mission. Surely I must be a masterful visioncaster to motivate people to go all over the world like that. It's assumed that we have a mission statement that clearly spells out our intent on starting churches. It could never happen without a very effective system of training for the church planters, right?

My twenty-three-year-old daughter, who has been part of this church from its inception, was in the room when I was asked this question. I felt that she would provide the dose of reality and authenticity that would be needed for the questioner to fathom my answer, so I first asked her, "Erin, during the lifetime of this church, when is the last time you heard me mention church planting or reaching out to people in this group?" You could sense the wheels in her head spinning to access her memories. She then replied, "Not for at least ten years."

Does that shock you? It should if you have been slaving away casting vision to your church for many years and not seen a whole lot of outreach. Most of the literature on revitalization of churches stress that outreach is important and then the prescription that follows is usually to cast vision, teach, and preach, telling stories of successful evangelism and provide training and new strategies. We pastors try to woo, inspire, challenge, guilt, and shame people into mission, and in the end we see little done. I do none of those things, and the result is tons of mission.

Let me be very clear: it is not the model of doing church that accounts for this extraordinary reproductive capacity. No, there are many house churches that do not reproduce. Our secret is not in the model, the agenda, the vision, the strategy, or the leadership. You will find the secret in the disciples themselves—in the DNA.

There are many churches that work hard to reproduce, and they do not have nearly as many daughters and granddaughters as this one little church that doesn't even have a budget for missions. I don't tell these people to reach out to others; they tell me about the people they are reaching out to. I don't have to tell them to pray for the lost because they are already praying every day for their lost friends and family. Most often I find out about a new church plant after it has already happened. There is a term for this in missiological language: *spontaneous growth.* We all say we want spontaneous growth, but too often we do not see it happen because we are putting more faith in our strategies, sermons, methods, conferences, and passionate appeals to allow for what really causes spontaneous growth to occur. In fact, much of our current methodology not only doesn't produce spontaneous growth but works against it.

METHODS THAT DON'T MULTIPLY

Churches use many methods in their attempts to multiply.

THE FRANCHISE MODEL

There is a church that we know of that once planted many churches all over the world. To its credit, it had even planted a few churches in its own city less than fifteen minutes away. One of its daughter churches, however, made the mistake of growing three to five times larger than the mother church, and it has done so using methods that are less than favorable in the eyes of the mother church. The result is that the original mother church stopped planting other churches. I (Neil) actually heard the leaders say that they didn't want to plant any more churches if they could possibly turn out like that one. Consequently, they decided to only plant churches that were guaranteed to look and function like the mother church. It has now been nearly twenty years since that church started any other churches.

There are many churches that are so in love with themselves that they believe the world needs more churches just like them. They franchise their church with its own brand so that people will know exactly what they will get if they go there, much like McDonald's or Starbucks.

Franchising is a business concept, not an organic one. You can franchise a Taco Bell but not a person. The idea of franchising churches is further evidence of how far afield our ecclesiology has drifted.

Aside from the egotistical business mind-set that produces consumers seeking a specific brand of Churchianity, this method will never lead to spontaneous multiplication. In biological terminology the closest thing we can find to franchising is *cloning*. I've watched enough *Star Trek* episodes to know that pure clones cannot reproduce by themselves. Of course, you may not consider *Star Trek* to be a credible enough source for you. It wasn't for me, so I asked a real expert. My sister has a Ph.D. in molecular biology and specializes in reproductive science, so I asked her if clones can reproduce. She said no and then gave me a scientific theory for why that blew right over my head. Suffice it to say that the expert, trained at MIT, told me that clones can't reproduce themselves.

If you want my own expert theological opinion why clones don't reproduce I will tell you: God is smart and we are stupid. How's that? Wow, my answer alone verifies half of the premise, doesn't it? You see, God is a creative deity who delights in the beauty of diversity; he made around 270,000 varieties of flowers with over one hundred different species of roses alone, if that tells you anything! I think he also realized that with our prideful worldview that somebody would somehow think the world a better place if there were more people "just like me." So fortunately God pre-empted that whole idea by making clones unable to reproduce. OK, maybe it's obvious now that my sister landed in the deep end of our genetic pool and I'm still in the shallow end, but I kind of like my simple answer.

Now I am very grateful that there is one kind of natural "clone" that can reproduce: the identical twin. But this is something God does, and I am glad that identical twins can reproduce because my own father is an identical twin! Where would I be if they couldn't reproduce? Now there's a question for the deep end!

Dolly, the first cloned sheep, cost an estimated $750,000 to $800,000 and died prematurely. Cloning takes effort, intentionality, strategy, lots of money, and a whole lot of ego. Frankly, we don't need more of you, but we always need something fresh and new. Cloning or franchising is merely an addition strategy at best. Stop trying to clone yourself.

God designed reproduction in such a way that every person in all the world, in all of human history for that matter—is unique. A child may have certain qualities that reflect his or her mother or father, but no child looks exactly like his or her parent. Each new person is a unique combination of genetic material from two very different people, and even if the couple are competing with the Duggars in the propagation sweepstakes, each person born to them will be a special, one-of-a-kind individual (even if they are identical twins). We need to follow God's beautiful and natural design for reproduction and fill the world with unique and diverse beauty.

THE DIVISION = MULTIPLICATION METHOD

A couple of decades ago some church growth gurus began teaching churches how to reproduce small groups, cell groups, or metachurches. Taking their cues from the mega-megachurches (now called gigachurches) of South Korea, they taught very complex systems with multicolored hemispheres and strange-sounding roles based on math.[1] I (Neil) remember reading the books with great enthusiasm and then trying to implement the complex ideas in frustration.

The problem is that they got the math wrong. They didn't teach us how to *multiply* but how to *divide*. Even I know there is a difference. The accompanying figure will picture for you the strategy they suggested for "multiplication." The strategy called for each group to start with a leader and an apprentice. The group would leave an empty chair in the room to remind all that there are others who need to be invited in (if empty chairs in church meetings ever really led people to Christ, we would be seeing revival all across the nation). As the group grew to a certain point (usually it is suggested that fifteen people attending is the point of division), the group would divide, the leader keeping half and the apprentice taking the other half. The problem that everyone ran into is that the people in the group felt like they were having their relationships severed randomly. It felt more like they were having a divorce than reproducing naturally.

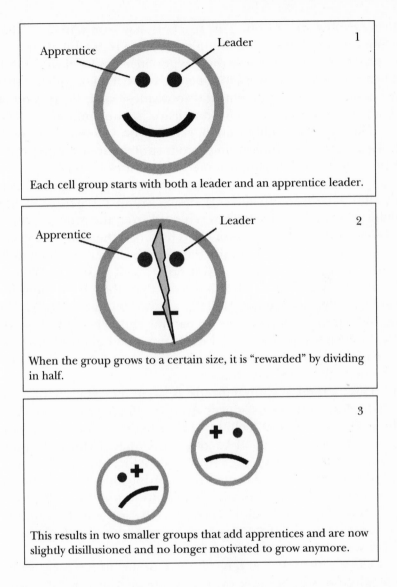

Each cell group starts with both a leader and an apprentice leader.

When the group grows to a certain size, it is "rewarded" by dividing in half.

This results in two smaller groups that add apprentices and are now slightly disillusioned and no longer motivated to grow anymore.

For many people this method of "multiplying," which is actually division, makes the idea of multiplication repugnant. I have found that wherever I teach on multiplication of groups, I face people who have been burned by this "divisive" method. It feels to many like they were finally given the opportunity to form real relationships in church and suddenly and seemingly randomly those relationships are cut off. This teaching has so proliferated that when you simply mention multiplication to a room full of church-goers, some cringe because their experience has been so painful. This method doesn't work for many reasons, least of which is that we don't need to be taught how to divide—we've been good at that for centuries now. We need to learn how to multiply.

This type of multiplication via division doesn't feel good. It feels more like divorce than reproduction because relationships feel severed unnaturally by some dictate from leadership in the church organization. This is just not natural reproduction, which should come from an internal desire within the people rather than a dictate from leadership removed from the group.

I will often ask a group of churchgoers if they have children, and usually a majority will raise their hands. I then say, "Oh, well, you know how to reproduce; you don't need to see that Power-Point." They usually laugh when I say that; then I tell them it's best that they not see *that* film clip anyway. But the reality is that reproduction is supposed to be natural and actually feel good! The conception part at least; I don't mean to minimize the pain of childbirth. We reproduce because we want to, not because someone tells us we have to.

This method of church growth is based on cellular biology: a cell divides and thus reproduces. Applying this to groups, however, doesn't work well. The "cell" of Christ's body is not a small group but a disciple in relation to other disciples. Cellular division occurs at the smallest level of a body's life, not in the more complex formations of the body. Applying this to churches or even small groups implies that the way to reproduce is to cut off a limb of the body, stick in a pot of soil, and wait for another human to develop. If this was how we reproduced as a species, I think we would all choose extinction.

Actually, the way real reproduction occurs in the body is that a single disciple, because of love, gives his life (his DNA—his Jesus) to another. When the disciples are doing this, the small groups and churches will find reproduction a whole lot easier.

The truth is that if the people in your church don't want to reproduce, you are unlikely to reproduce your church, and no amount of chiding or enthusiastic pep talks will make it happen. In such a case, the problem is a DNA issue.

THE SATELLITE CHURCH MODEL

One change that is sweeping through the Western church today is the multisite model, whereby one church spins off several branches, venues, or sites. This phenomenon is so popular that a recent book by Geoff Surratt, Greg Ligon, and Warren Bird called *A Multi-Site Church Road Trip* has the audacious subtitle *Exploring the New Normal.*[2] According to their book, on a typical Sunday in 2009, some five million people—almost 10 percent of Protestant worshipers—attended a multisite church in the United States or Canada. Leaders at some 45,000 churches are seriously considering the multisite approach, according to a recent survey by LifeWay Research. Before you jump on the bandwagon, we want you to think about a few things.

What does it mean to be a multisite church? Basically, it is one church meeting in more than one location. Some use the term *campuses* or *services;* others call them *satellite churches, polysites,* or even *house churches* or *missional communities.*

There are, of course, variations on this theme. Some are video venues where different styles of worship are offered at different sites or in different rooms, sometimes even on the same campus. The same sermon from the same preacher is usually beamed in to them all on a larger-than-life screen. Some are spread across a city while others branch out across a state and a few have even gone interstate. Some are on the Internet; a few are even branching out internationally. For some people it is a way to grow their church when there is no possibility of building a larger facility. For others it is a way of building a network of churches. Many people like it because they can have church for a variety of different tastes. Some even call it church planting, but others say that it is counterfeit church planting.

I have friends who used to start lots of churches and lately they have resorted instead to starting video venue services with their own sermons beamed in. To call that a church plant, in my opinion, cheapens missiology. Whereas they used to spend a great deal of time training new church planters, they now train campus pastors, and there is a difference. It is no longer necessary to train preachers, visionaries, or entrepreneurial leaders because the lead pastor can have his sermons beamed in to every venue. A strong leader is not as desired as a good manager in starting new campus sites. Even the vision is developed and cast by the lead pastor; the campus pastor simply finds ways to pass it on. This is not church planting as we have known it; it is worship service addition. Addition is not bad, it is certainly better than subtraction or division, but it is not multiplication.

A few satellite church venues have actually initiated others to date, but the number of these "grandchildren" is very few, and the reproduction is actually very slow when compared to a true church planting movement.

Surratt, Ligon, and Warren have pointed out in their book about six or so "grandchildren" campuses of the multisite "revolution" across the country.[3] To date there is not any evidence of a fourth-generation church plant or campus. It is notable that of three thousand multisite churches with two or more campuses that the book identifies, with tens of thousands of services, fewer than ten grandchildren can be identified in the United States. This should be enough evidence to challenge the idea that multisite multiplies.

In the book, Surratt and colleagues state that it is grandchildren that sustain and give legs to a movement, but we argue that it is the fourth generation, or great-grandchildren, that are the true evidence of multiplication and hence a movement. The multisite model is very far removed from seeing this. Currently, this model has only a 1 percent reproductive rate. This is not enough to maintain any species, so we do not put great hope in this burgeoning movement. We believe it will never become a multiplication movement because there are too many values inherent within it that prevent true multiplication from happening. Primary among those is the dependence on the main preacher in a consumer-oriented environment and the subsequent weakening view that church is nothing more than a worship service.

TRUE SPONTANEOUS MULTIPLICATION

I (Neil) have written more than my share on the subject of multiplication, so I'll not repeat all of it here. What I do want to focus on here is the idea of *spontaneous* multiplication. What I described at the start of this chapter is spontaneous multiplication;

it happens all by itself. Jesus told an important parable of how the kingdom of God grows. In it He says that a farmer sows the seed and goes to sleep by night and wakes up by day, and the seed sprouts and grows all by itself. The Greek word translated as "all by itself" is *automate*. We need to understand that inherent in the DNA of God's kingdom is the power to spawn automatic growth. As long as we are focused on making things grow, we will lose this powerful and beautiful element of God's kingdom—spontaneous growth.

I remember when I was first seeing spontaneous multiplication occur while I was pastoring a conventional established church. I was so excited because I had been waiting my whole life to see it. One group multiplied into three others, and I never instructed them to do it. They did it all by themselves! Then more followed. This is what spontaneous reproduction looks like.

I was still a product of the traditional Christian leadership system, so I did what seemed natural to me: I cast vision for multiplication every chance I got. Even though things were clicking and multiplying without permission or program, I was fearful that we might start losing momentum, so I cranked up the vision casting. Then I got a negative reaction. A couple of women came up to me and told me they wished I would stop talking about multiplying. They finally had a group that they liked and didn't want to split it up. Does that sound familiar? Because one of the women was my wife, I listened to them.

I felt the Spirit tell me that if indeed the seed of God's Word (DNA) was being planted in good soil (a willing heart), I did not need to cast vision. The impetus for real organic reproduction is not from the outside but from the inside. So I decided to put this to the test. I told the women that they were right. I would stop casting vision for reproduction and grant them permission *not* to reproduce. I stopped enforcing reproduction as a plan and simply let God do what only God can do. Three months later that women's group had become three, spontaneously.

This does reveal a problem we all run into. We all tend to think we need to help the gospel. We would never admit it, but this is revealed by our actions. We actually place more faith in our methods and messages than in the message of God.

We simply must believe in the seed of God's Word, plant it, and let it do what only it can do. You must make a choice. Do you cause the reproduction or does God? It's a choice of faith, and if you choose wrongly, you will find yourself working very hard for a very long time with little or no reproductive fruit to show for it. Sorry, but that is the truth. On the other hand, if you believe in the spontaneity of organic reproduction, your life will become much easier. Instead of trying to motivate the unmotivated or create life where there is none, you can simply cast the seed broadly and water where you see the growth. The DNA empowered by the Spirit of God will do the rest of the work.

George Patterson, speaking about spontaneous reproduction, wrote:

> Every time we eat, we eat the fruit of God's tremendous reproduction power given to plants and animals. Look around out of doors; it's everywhere—grass, trees, birds, bees, babies, and flowers. All creation is shouting it! This is the way God works! . . . We ourselves don't make the church grow or reproduce, any more than pulling on a stalk of corn would make it grow.[4]

All reproduction starts at the smallest level possible. We must reproduce disciples first, as we have already discussed at length. If we can't reproduce disciples, we will never see spontaneous reproduction of leaders. If leaders do not reproduce, we will never see churches reproduce all by themselves. Immediately following the parable of automatic growth, Jesus told another one saying the kingdom starts with the smallest seed, the mustard seed.

The parable of the mustard seed teaches us that the spread of God's kingdom starts simply and small but steadily grows to become more and more complex. The power of multiplication works in a similar way. If we focus on reproducing disciples who reproduce disciples who carry the DNA of Jesus, we will ignite a movement that multiplies exponentially.

RAPID REPRODUCTION

According to David Garrison, author of the seminal book *Church Planting Movements*, one of the ten characteristics of a church planting movement is rapid reproduction.[5] Because many people do not see reproduction occurring rapidly, they have taken issue with this assessment. Actually, if you are truly multiplying, rapid is the only way—eventually. All multiplication begins slow and small and builds toward rapid momentum over time. That is sound arithmetic, and you must respect both the slow and small start as well as the rapid exponential up-curve that eventually comes. That is how movements emerge. In a sense you must have both if it is to be an exponential movement—the slow, small start and the rapid exponential momentum later. Do not despise the day of small beginnings, but don't stay there either.

We've heard a few people argue against spontaneous and rapid reproduction of churches and the consequent movements that we believe will occur. One metaphorical argument is that it takes years for a girl to mature to the point where she can reproduce. Another argument is that a tree doesn't bear fruit for several years while it grows and matures.

We think using an analogy of a girl or a tree to prove that a church cannot mature to a place of reproducing quickly is not a sound biblical argument. Leaven multiplies quickly and is an actual analogy that Jesus used; a girl is not. A single shaft of wheat allowed to reproduce freely and multiply for several generations will have multiplied enough within only eight years to feed the entire world population for a year. Did Jesus ever use wheat as an analogy of multiplication? Yes, He did. He used the analogy of a tree only when he was describing the genetic properties that produce the correct kind of fruit. "A good tree will produce good fruit, and a bad tree will produce bad fruit." Ironically, He also used a tree as an analogy to describe the frustration inherent when there is a lack of reproduction (Luke 13:6–9). When he wanted to speak of multiplication, and specifically of rapidity, he spoke of leaven and wheat. But even if you speak of human beings, the truth is that the population of the planet is increasing at an exponential rate. No one can argue that the population is rapidly multiplying and increasing in that momentum every decade.

ROADBLOCKS TO REPRODUCTION

In *Church 3.0,* Neil mentions three consistent roadblocks to church multiplication and reproduction: buildings, budgets, and big shots.[6]

Buildings are not bad or wrong; they are simply not alive and therefore cannot reproduce. Buildings usually cost an exorbitant amount of money to purchase and even more to maintain. But perhaps the worst part about buildings is that they claim our love and ultimately our devotion. They anchor us in one place and become missional black holes. This has been the status quo for so long that our buildings have actually become synonymous with church in our minds and the minds of the people we are trying to reach. Our language has fused church with a building, revealing that our hearts have melded them together.

Budgets can keep us from reproducing. If it costs a lot to start a church, then it stands to reason that fewer churches will be initiated because the newer church will not have the financial wherewithal to repeat the pattern established by the mother church. If your church has a large budget, you might be tempted to think you have greater resources to apply toward multiplying, but actually you have a greater hindrance to reproduction. The more a church costs, the less likely it will reproduce.

Big shots—key leaders who carry the weight of all the leadership—curtail reproduction when they are seen as needed for the church. Dependence on big names or prominent clergy does two very sinister things: it dulls regular Christians, and it exalts a few to higher status and importance in the church. Both of these outcomes curtail all reproduction from the start. This is not to say that dynamic leadership is not useful in a movement but that the formation and reproduction of the church cannot be carried by the personality of one person. If it is, there will never be multiplication, just addition. Leadership in a movement is more about influencing influencers than it is about being the one who is the "face" of the church. For instance, if the vision comes from one person and is carried out by others, that creates a dependence that curtails true reproduction. Sound leadership in a movement is not coming up with the vision and then casting it to others but instead is about helping others find a vision for themselves and releasing them to fulfill it. This should happen over and over again to the ends of the earth.

Grandparenting Movements

The truth is that most established churches will be unable to multiply spontaneously. They have become too complex and too expensive to reproduce spontaneously. Real spontaneous reproduction occurs on the micro level. Spontaneously reproducing an established church with property and a professional staff is just not going to happen.

Take an honest look at your own church. If it is over a hundred people and has a building and a professional pastor or two, it is already well beyond the size from which it can spontaneously multiply. You'll also not spontaneously multiply if your model of church is currently built on addition strategies and is too expensive and too complicated. A second Saddleback church is not going to just spontaneously pop up in Orange County. But this doesn't take away the possibility of your church birthing movements; you simply have to look further down the line. Instead of trying to reproduce your current highly complex church, we suggest that you consider grandparenting movements by allowing something very different to be born out of your church, something that can actually multiply spontaneously. This can be done. Los Altos Grace Brethren Church has done this numerous times.

One final reason that I suspect many churches are not reproducing is because, frankly, God doesn't want more of them. The truth is that many of our churches are not healthy. Why would God want to fill the earth with anemic and immature followers?

At the bottom of the whole issue of the lack of reproduction is a discipleship problem. We need to develop disciples that are so in love with Jesus that they simply can't stay put in the status quo any longer but are compelled by love to tell their neighbors and the nations about the Jesus they love. That is the sort of church that will multiply; it is the sort of church that God will want more of.

Multiplication and Death

Reproduction always occurs at the microscopic level, even in your own body right now. The hand that is holding this book is made up of millions of cells, and each is multiplying. Your entire body is being replaced by new cells all the time—that is health. Every few months there is a new you! In order for your body to continue to regenerate itself in this manner, old cells must die for new ones to be born.

Imagine what would happen if the cells in your hand decided to stop multiplying. The moment your cells stop multiplying, you have a serious problem on your hands (pardon the pun). Your hand will shrivel up and die. Or imagine what would happen if your cells continually reproduced without any of them dying. You would become a giant and be unfit for this world.

Multiplication of cells stops only when death occurs. At the same time, death occurs when multiplication stops. Both statements are true. Death and multiplication are intricately woven together in a symbiotic relationship.

While it may sound paradoxical, there is also a spiritual truth that multiplication starts with death. There is a cost involved in multiplication. For the salmon, the cost is death. It swims upstream, lays its eggs in the sand, and then dies. It lives to multiply. It dies to multiply.

Grain also dies to reproduce. Jesus said, "Truly, truly, I say to you, unless a grain of wheat falls into the earth and dies, it remains by itself alone; but if it dies, it bears much fruit. He who loves his life loses it; and he who hates his life in this world shall keep it to life eternal" (John 12:24).

As disciples, we must deny ourselves, pick up our cross, and follow Christ. This is all about surrender. This is about confession and repentance. This is about obedience. Where these things exist there is a dying of self, and generation upon generation of new growth will be the result.

We've got to be willing to give up more than our time, talents, and treasure—we've got to start by giving up our *lives* for the sake of His kingdom. If we are willing to pay the price—if we are willing to die to follow Christ—then we can see an abundant harvest of souls for the kingdom of God. The Christians of the first century were willing to give their lives for the expansion of the kingdom, and they were able to reach the entire known world with the gospel. Every church throughout history whose members were willing to surrender their lives for the sake of Christ witnessed dramatic and spontaneous growth. This is one reason why churches thrive under persecution—the people of God are forced to decide what really matters most. They count the cost and pay the price. They die to themselves, their spiritual lives reproduce, and church growth occurs through multiplication.

When disciples die to themselves and live crucified lives in the world, the effect is far more influential than ministry remaining within the confines of a church building. The old standards of measuring success are limited to the bottom line for an institution. If your church transfuses and releases healthy disciples to reproduce, new standards of measurement will be needed, and Chapter Twelve will address that issue.

CHAPTER TWELVE

NEW MEASURES
OF SUCCESS

It used to be so easy to determine who was successful and who was not. Bigger was assumed to be better. We simply counted the people attending and the dollars given and we knew if we were successful or not. Those days are quickly ending, and those standards never were an accurate measure of real success in any case.

In *Church 3.0* Neil writes:

> In Church 2.0 we evaluated a church's success by how many people attended and how much money they left there. Because Church 3.0 is a movement, success is not measured by how many people come but by how many go! We want to measure the church's sending capacity more than its seating capacity. We ask: Is the message, the method and the mission spreading from one person to the next and then on to the one after that?[1]

Our mission is to find and develop Christ followers rather than church members. There is a big difference. The difference is seen in transformed lives that bring change to neighborhoods and nations. Simply gathering a group of people who subscribe to a common set of beliefs is not worthy of Jesus and the sacrifice He made for us.

We must shift from institutional measures to measures of influence. Instead of the numbers question, we must look for the personal influence of the real church—the people who make up the spiritual family in whatever place they are found. If church is not an event but a family, then we need to measure a family's success rather than an event's, and the two are measured very differently. In a family we measure maturity, direction, stories, and uniqueness. Each person in a healthy family is measured against his or her own potential and past accomplishments, not against other siblings. In a family, success is seen generationally; we think about children, grandchildren, and a legacy left to the generations that follow.

Many people ask for benchmarks to measure the success of the organization, as if that is measuring the church. It is not. The church is not the building, the organization, the programs, or the events. You can measure all those things and still not measure the success or failure of the church because the church is something else entirely. As Reggie McNeal likes to say, "Church is not a 'what' but a 'who.'"[2] The church is disciples in relationship together on a mission—surrendering to Jesus and allowing Him to influence the world through them. Once you factor that simple shift into the mix, the entire equation changes. How do you measure the influence of a person in relation to other people? This is a far better barometer of how we are doing as a church or a movement. As Neil says in *Organic Church*:

> Church attendance is not the barometer of how Christianity is doing. Ultimately, transformation is the product of the Gospel. It is not enough to fill our churches; we must transform our world. Society and culture should change if the church has been truly effective. Is the church reaching out and seeing lives changed by the Good News of the Kingdom of God? Surely the numbers of Christians will increase once this happens, but filling seats one day a week is not what the Kingdom is all about. We do Jesus an injustice by reducing His life and ministry to such a sad story as church attendance and membership roles. The measure of the church's influence is found in society—on the streets, not in the pews.[3]

We lost count of the number of churches in our movement years ago. You cannot measure numbers of churches in a multiplication movement, except perhaps in the beginning, when 2 becomes 4 and 4 becomes 8 and so on. Even with our mathematically challenged minds we can do that. In an addition strategy, measuring success by counting people and churches is easy. But as the exponential growth curve rises, old means of measurement become useless.

In *The Starfish and the Spider*, Ori Brafman and Rod Beckstrom say:

> Counting the members of starfish organizations (decentralized organizations) is usually an impossible task. It's not only that no one's keeping track, but also that anyone can become a member of an open organization—or likewise withdraw their membership—at any time.[4]

As we say at CMA, "If you are successful in a church multiplication movement, then you can't count the number of churches. If you can count the churches, then you are not experiencing a multiplication movement."[5] How's that for a measuring stick? Your success is determined by *not* counting. It reverses the whole conversation, doesn't it?

But we are human, so we still want to know how we are doing. Success for the church is measured on the streets, not in the seats. We measure human interaction and transformative stories. We are very proud of some of the work done by one of our associated ministries in our hometown of Long Beach, California. Due in large part to the efforts of Kingdom Causes LB, homelessness has been reduced by more than 25 percent. That is success in anyone's book, but could that happen if we were content to merely count butts in seats and 10 percent of the dollars found in the wallets in the pockets on those butts?

What happens when we celebrate things that don't matter and ignore the ones that do? Neil asked that very question on his Facebook page once and received a ton of interesting responses. Perhaps the saddest was the simple reply "You get church." Ouch.

We fuel what we celebrate. When we turn inward and hide away in our own little bubble, we lose touch with reality. We become deluded into a selfish consumerism, content with passive opinions that count for little more than the whining of a spoiled child. Our true north is lost, and we spiral into a deeper and deeper level of deception as we invest more and more in what we unwittingly think is success. We think we are doing well when in fact we long ago took the off ramp from God's true missional agenda and are now lost in a maze of new programs designed for ourselves and for our own organizational prosperity. The extent of our self-deception is enormous.

Jesus, of course would not be considered a success by our errant standards of measure, as he left behind only 120 disciples (Acts 1:15). Apparently he neglected to attend the "How to Break the 200 Growth Barrier" seminar. But he was never interested in large numbers of people coming; he was interested in a few that would go, be fruitful, and multiply. This approach eventually rose to overcome the Roman Empire when no other strategy could.

From Institutional to Influential Success in Acts

When it comes to measuring impact, a transition that occurs in the book of Acts is worth noting. In the early chapters, success was measured in precise numbers that were added to the growing local church (Acts 2:41, 5:41). Later the success was measured by how "the Word of the Lord was being spread through the whole region" (Acts 13:49). Once the church transitioned to become a more organic decentralized movement, success was measured by how many churches were growing stronger in faith and being added to the movement on a daily basis (Acts 16:5). Eventually, when it became a rapidly multiplying movement, success was measured by the fact that "all who were in Asia heard the Word of the Lord, both Jews and Greeks" (Acts 19:20).

Did you catch that? It doesn't just say that the Word could be found in every place of Asia, as if the Gideons were there and left a free Bible in the nightstand (as incredible as that would be). It says that every person who was in Asia—Jew or Greek, man, woman, or child—had heard God's message. The Lord's voice was heard by everyone! Talk about reaching a people group! It doesn't tell us how many responded positively to that message, only that they heard it. In fact, we know that many responded very negatively (1 Cor. 16:9).

In a rapid exponentially building movement, measurement takes on a whole different form. As our good friend and coworker Ed Waken likes to say, "It is not how many conversions are made but how many conversations people have." It is connections with the people that are measured, which is actually something we can intentionally invest in. The results of those conversations are not measured because, frankly, that is not our success or failure. We cannot control that or take credit for it. We plant the seeds; God makes them grow.

Unfortunately, we tend to measure things that are outside of our realm of control. When we claim success by counting the number of conversions we have seen, we are claiming success for something only God can do. People will willingly admit that only Jesus saves people but then congratulate themselves for the number of salvations that occur under their ministry. This reflects a clear disconnect between their theology and practice.

Paul scolds the Corinthian church for the pride it felt over the use of its spiritual gifts. The church of Corinth had divided into groups based on being the fruit of a particular spiritual leader, either Paul or Apollos (1 Cor. 3:1–4). Paul goes on to say, "Why do you boast over that which is a gift received?" (1 Cor. 4:6–7). In other words, if you could do the work without the gift, you may have reason to boast, but the very fact that you need a special gift to accomplish the work is testimony of how incapable you actually are.

We have a tendency to take or give credit for things that are not ours to claim or assign. This is a serious problem for us today in the church, just as it was in Corinth. We align with certain leaders' "success" based on response to their message, as if their sermons saved people rather than Jesus. Instead of saying, "I am of Paul" or "I am of Apollos," we have people saying, "I am of Rick Warren" or "I am of Mark Drischol." We go even further to add our brands to ministry, and then people align with that ministry or not: "I am of IHOP" versus "I am of 24/7 Prayer." This is foolishness. The body ends up turning against itself in competition for a share of the Christian market and then congratulates itself for how many more people it has than the others.

In that same paragraph where he claims that we ought not boast over what is received as a gift, Paul writes about how foolish it is to align with one Christian leader over another because of what appears to be success. He says, "So that in us you may learn not to *exceed what is written,* so that no one of you will become arrogant in behalf of one against the other" (emphasis mine). He is specifically addressing the very thing we are writing about in this chapter. There is a disconnect between what is written in the Scriptures and how we measure success in our churches.

We are not responsible for our own salvation, let alone the salvation of others; we never have been and never will be. Our responsibility is to bring the presence, power, and voice—in other words, personal influence—of our King to places where He is not being seen, heard, or felt. We need to let Him do what only He can do and let Him get credit for the results. Frankly, Jesus can do a whole lot more than just get people to show up for an hour-long event once a week. His influence is over every area of our lives, which makes measurement with precise numbers seem trite and minimal in the end.

To claim institutional success, objective proof that we have reached our stated goal as an organization is needed. This again betrays our misunderstanding that the church is an organization formed to accomplish tasks instead of a living thing created to grow and multiply. This misconception causes us to believe that proof marked and measured by a business mind-set that feeds some bottom line is the mark of the organization's success or failure. The problem is that the kingdom is not meant to be a business or an organization. It is the reign of the King in the hearts of ordinary people who are being transformed into agents of extraordinary influence. It is this personal influence, one life touching another, that we believe builds into the momentum of a movement. The kingdom brings change; it transforms our entire life, for our entire life. Such transformation is obvious and easily noted but not quantitatively measurable with statistical analysis. And it is never complete, so success is not something that can be achieved until the end. This is why the apostle Paul could commend the Thessalonians for their love and at the same time encourage them to "excel still more"(1 Thess. 4:1).

We can measure process or even progress but not true success until the end. We all have the potential to fail and disqualify ourselves at any moment, and the only exam that actually counts is the final exam. Likewise, the only applause that really counts is the applause at the finish line. Any applause before that is encouraging but not truly satisfying.

As we say in our movement, "You don't graduate until there is a flat line on the monitor next to your bed." Until then you keep learning, growing, and moving forward toward the upward call of God in Christ Jesus. We need to finish well or die trying.

So influential success is measured moment to moment and is more about stories of changed lives than numbers of people present.

NOT ALWAYS ABOUT POSITIVE RESULTS

It's not how many walk an aisle on Sunday in church that measures success but how many walk with Jesus in the world every day. For far too long the church has been afraid of the world and the effect the world would have on it. In contrast, mission-minded people choose to have an effect on the world, not the other way around.

Institutional success measures attendance and budgets. Influential success measures the presence and resulting impact of our being in the world and bringing the voice of our King. In a sense, even the rejection of that influence is a sign of our success. The type of response the message receives is not within our control and never was. All we are responsible for is spreading the voice of Jesus to people; what they do with that message is completely up to them.

In a real sense, it is not our attendance charts, year-end reports, and newsletters that tell of our success; often it is the voice of those who are not even in the church and may never darken its doorway. Sometimes the indicator of success sounds more like an insult. Look at how Luke describes Paul and his band of missional disciples in Acts through the eyes of those steeped in the world system:

> And when they had brought them to the chief magistrates, they said, "These men are throwing our city into confusion." [Acts 16:20]
>
> They began dragging Jason and some brethren before the city authorities, shouting, "These men who have upset the world have

come here also; and Jason has welcomed them, and they all act contrary to the decrees of Caesar, saying that there is another king, Jesus." [Acts 17:6–7]

You see and hear that not only in Ephesus, but in almost all of Asia, this Paul has persuaded and turned away a considerable number of people, saying that gods made with hands are no gods at all. [Acts 19:26]

These are entirely different measures of success for the church than what we usually tally. Granted, we Christians hardly need excuses to be more offensive to the world than we already are. That's not the point, but when we actually mobilize God's people into the thick of the marketplace and the world system, the true enemy will not respond softly. When we keep people sidelined in comfy sanctuaries, the devil is hardly threatened.

Lobbying Congress for a more conservative political agenda is hardly what our true purpose is; yet that is what the world sees of us. Jesus never did that, even though the people He was serving would have preferred that He do so. Instead, He simply transformed people and empowered them to make a difference in their portion of the world. The people He really insulted and offended were the highly conservative religious leaders. As we mentioned in Chapter One, Al and Deb Hirsch ask a profound couple of questions in their book *Untamed*:

What is it about the holiness of Jesus that caused "sinners" to flock to him like a magnet and yet manages to seriously antagonize the religious people? This question begs yet another, even more confronting question: why does our more churchy form of holiness seem to get it the other way around?[6]

Is it possible that we are too nice to the wrong people and too mean to the right ones? Jesus shocked his foes, his friends, and his followers in equal doses. Although it was the Romans who crucified Jesus, it was the leaders of His own religious faith who instigated the persecution and demanded the outcome. That is fairly consistent with radical spiritual revolutionaries. Ask any soldier or radical change agent: "friendly fire" isn't so friendly.

We believe that an indicator of influential success is determined by whom you anger and whom you do not. We think this barometer does not indicate that the church in America is doing very well in terms of influential success. As a result, we experience very little real persecution.

Perhaps we are so rarely truly persecuted because we so rarely threaten to shake things up out in the world where we are really needed. Jesus promised that if they persecuted Him, they would also do so to us. Paul wrote that all who desire to live godly will be persecuted. Perhaps we are not persecuted because we are not being like Jesus and are not living the sort of godly lives that would merit such. Why would Satan persecute a church that has voluntarily taken itself out of the action and off the field where it could actually do some good?

"I get it!" came a remark from a pastor in one of Reggie McNeal's D.Min. classes.

"I have been thinking all along about changing the church. You are talking about changing the world!"

Reggie concludes, "He did get it!"[7]

We have got to set our sights on something much bigger than a church with thousands in weekly attendance. Contrary to what you thought, changing the church is not the idea of this book no matter what the subtitle claims. That is a small goal not worth fulfilling. We need to change the world. Anything less is demeaning of Christ's sacrifice. As Leonard Sweet has said, "Can the church stop its puny, hack dreams of trying to 'make a difference in the world' and start dreaming God-sized dreams of making the world different?"[8]

LONG LIVE THE ORGANIC CHURCH

My (Neil's) wife is very health-conscious and buys groceries at places that sell organic food. I found out quickly that organic groceries go bad more quickly than those that contain artificial preservatives. Is that true for all things organic, even churches? Will our movement eventually die? Is there an expiration date on the church whose life is organic?

Mark Galli published an article in *Christianity Today* titled "Long Live Organic Church!"[9] In it he expresses some admiration but also concern for the well-being of some of the thought leaders of the organic church movement. He implies that the bitter disappointment of seeing the inevitable failure of our movement may cause us to become bitter and fall out of service to God altogether.

The concerns he expresses are not just valid; they are haunting realizations we have lived with for over a decade. Sustainability, longevity, and the threat of institutionalization are all subjects we have thought about considerably. But holding unreal expectations and the disillusionment that can result has not ever been a concern of ours.

We do not live for success but to follow Christ every day. If when our lives end we have only a handful of followers of Jesus that can carry on His work, we will not be ashamed to meet our Lord, who left much the same behind. In 2 Timothy 4, Paul was in the same place, but he said he finished the course and kept the faith. He also transformed the world! He planted seeds that bore fruit for generations to come. There were some things put in place that would bring lasting change throughout the centuries. There were other things that lasted only a generation or two. We think that is the way of true awakenings. Some new ideas stick forever, others only for a time.

Our friend, Bob Logan, has said numerous times, "Success is finding out what God wants you to do and then doing it." We think that is really the truth. As long as there is a living and loving God, this success is available to us all.

CAN WE CHANGE THE WORLD?

Is transformation of society the true mark of a movement? We think it is. As we have said to many who question our legitimacy, it is not our contemporary experts and critics who will give us our validity but future historians. We often think of future historians and their perspective when we look at things; it helps us gain a bigger and broader perspective of the here and now. We also recommend highly that you do as well. When you want to measure how you and your church are doing, ask what a historian would say one hundred years from now. Would a future historian even notice your church? If so, what would the historian connect to your church that grants it attention? We are convinced that if we all did that, we would have a better perspective of what is important and what is not. We should be less concerned with our peers' perspective or our popularity within the church world and more with the probable conclusions of future hindsight.

Jesus commanded us to influence the world (Matt. 28:18–20). He described his movement as going to the ends of the earth (Acts 1:8) until the end of the age (Matt. 28:20). He described the kingdom as a mustard seed that grows well beyond expectations into global influence (Matt. 13:31–32). He described His kingdom as leaven that spreads throughout the lump of dough and changes everything (Matt. 13:33–35). We will stake our lives on Jesus' intent rather than cower from other people's criticism and adopt their low expectations.

If we truly saturate our society with vital followers of Christ capable of making disciples, the world will change. We believe that simply connecting God's children to their spiritual Father in such a way that they listen to His voice and courageously follow His lead will transform society in broader, holistic, and longer-lasting ways than anything else we try.

The change, however, will not be for every generation. In fact, it could very well be that thinking the decisions we make today will be permanent causes our most insidious problems in the first place. We end up establishing methods that people will follow without hearing from God themselves and making their own choices of faith, and the result is that we create what we set out to avoid—a lifeless religious institution.

CAN WE CHANGE THE FUTURE?

Homer Simpson once said on *The Simpsons,* "I guess people never really change, or they quickly change and then quickly change back again." It feels like it's nearly impossible to find real lifelong change in people these days. In a real sense, however, all transformation is only momentary. There is a reason for this: we are called to live in the moment. Love is the fulfillment of all righteousness, and as we mentioned earlier, it is always a choice. We are to love God with our whole being every day. Who you are is really a lifetime of decisions made in specific moments. God wants us to choose him every moment of every day, not just once at a middle school retreat campfire. Love is a present-tense imperative. Love is always fulfilled today, now, or it is never fulfilled at all.

Each generation must face its own tests and make its own choice. Paul said of King David, "After he had served the purpose of God in his own generation, [he] fell asleep, and was laid among his fathers" (Acts 13:36). Even the patriarch David, though he left a lasting influence on every subsequent generation, could truly only fulfill his own God-given purpose within the time frame of his own life. This is all anyone is ever truly given. Life is like a coin; you can spend it any way you want, but you can only spend it once. After that, it is for someone else to spend.

Our children do not become Christians because we chose to follow Christ but because they do. If they are merely living out the choices of their parents, their faith is not true and will remain, at best, fruitless religious conformity. This is also true for religious organizations.

We are all mortals who strive to become immortal. We were meant to live forever in paradise, but because of the fall, death is a reality for us all. Throughout the ages, humankind has done all that it can to leave a mark on the world with some memorial so that our success will transcend death and be remembered throughout time. This mentality is also pervasive in the church. We want to leave behind something that will last for generations to come, and this leads us to make decisions on behalf of future generations. For instance, we set a policy or a practice that is meant to be followed by all subsequent generations. Although a significant decision that we make in our own time and context may be very meaningful, there is no guarantee that it will carry the same meaning twenty-five or thirty years from now. Future generations must face their own situation and make their own choices with their own faith. We cannot do that for them.

This type of legacy thinking is what leads a church into institutionalization and a type of slow death. Self-preservation of an organization, method, or idea for generations to come violates the faith of future followers and actually kills the very thing we try to keep alive by causing it to rely on something other than a vital faith. We need to trust Jesus as much with the future as we do with the present. He is the Alpha and Omega; He can take care of His church in the future as well as the past and the present. We all need to respect the faith of our children and let them own the choices that they must make.

What Can We Leave Behind for Future Generations?

○ *An example.* We have learned much by studying the lives of people like Paul, Count Zinzendorf, John Wesley, and Watchman Nee. Perhaps our grandchildren can study our lives and learn something to apply to their own generation. Hopefully, they won't mindlessly do what we did any more than selling tickets to a seat in the pew will work for us like it did for Wesley. The process of contextualizing truth for a new generation is dynamic and produces enlightened and influential leaders as well as better and more useful methods.

○ *Written enlightenment.* Many people today cite a book written a century ago by the Anglican missionary Roland Allen: *Missionary Methods: St Paul's or Ours?* When I (Neil) write, I think first about the immediate impact on a leader today, but I also wonder what relevance the book will have seventy-five years from now. I probably don't hit the second target very often (the first target is also debatable), but I do aim for it. We all stand on the broad shoulders of previous generations.

○ *Changes in cultural values and laws.* Sometimes the work of a few becomes the legacy to the many. Where once slavery was the norm for virtually millennia, today it is seen as an abomination because a few people, like Wilberforce and the Quakers, instigated a movement. Some changes in values do shape future culture. Our legacy can be more than a street named after us or a lecture hall on some college in the Midwest.

○ *Godly children.* Perhaps our greatest gift to the next generation is the next generation. We can give ourselves to them, unconditionally, and train them to think for themselves and follow Jesus at all costs. We can give them the freedom and responsibility to make the right choices, out of love for Jesus, rather than leave to them the policies of a previous generation.

When one tries to determine success, he or she simply must have a measuring rod, a standard to measure against. Unfortunately, today that measuring tape is often attendance and popularity, which is then compared against other people or churches. What we have tried to demonstrate in this chapter is that such an exercise is futile. The Corinthians struggled with a similar issue. They compared the success of Paul against others who were more outspoken and demanding of respect based upon their good speaking and popularity with others. Paul wrote:

> For we are not bold to class or compare ourselves with some of those who commend themselves; but when they measure themselves by themselves and compare themselves with themselves, they are without understanding. But we will not boast beyond our measure, but within the measure of the sphere which God apportioned to us as a measure, to reach even as far as you. For we are not overextending ourselves, as if we did not reach to you, for we were the first to come even as far as you in the gospel of Christ; not boasting beyond our measure, that is, in other men's labors, but with the hope that as your faith grows, we will be, within our sphere, enlarged even more by you, so as to preach the gospel even to the regions beyond you, and not to boast in what has been accomplished in the sphere of another. But he who boasts is to boast in the Lord. For it is not he who commends himself that is approved, but he whom the Lord commends. [2 Cor. 10:12–18]

We feel that making the list of top one hundred fastest growing or largest churches in America is not true success. Ambition to make such a list demonstrates a poor understanding of success. That amounts to measuring and commending ourselves against ourselves, which Paul says lacks understanding. We suggest instead that success is doing what Christ tells you and is best measured by how far the gospel is heard (geographically and in time/history). It can equally be measured by the response it receives whether positive or negative and the stories it produces in the lives of people, not numbers. But when we assume that we are responsible for the choices of others we cross a line that will lead to ruin in the long run. Ultimately it is not the organization or institution that must remain but the fruit of the gospel in people—transformed lives. We simply must stop measuring institutional success and then boasting about it, and instead, start looking for influential success.

As we have stated clearly we are not responsible for how people respond to the voice of Christ, we are only responsible for getting that voice out there. There are basically only three types of response: acceptance, apathy, and anger. There is a price to pay for becoming a church of influential success, and that is what Chapter Thirteen will address.

THE PRICE OF TRANSFUSION

At the end of our organic church training, which we call Greenhouse, we show a clip from the *Lord of the Rings* movies. It is a scene in which Sam explains his own revelation that the best stories, the ones that really matter, are always full of conflict. Good stories always involve darkness, doubt, and dread; that is what makes the story compelling, real, and worth telling. An epic battle of good versus evil is never easy and does not come without a steep cost. In this chapter we want to spell out some of that cost ahead of time so that you can move forward informed.

We've said much about the need for all disciples of Jesus to be willing to die to themselves in order to live for God. Nowhere is this more true than for those who find themselves in positions of leadership.

Change is a painful process. People get used to their surroundings and routines and become uncomfortable, even anxious or angry, when pushed to change them. It has taken decades, if not centuries, to evolve the unhealthy patterns and processes that permeate twenty-first-century Christianity. These weedlike patterns of thinking and living are deeply rooted and won't be easy to remove. The church leader who seeks to fulfill his or her calling to make and release disciples will be working at cross purposes with the status quo and will find that upsetting that apple cart will indeed upset everyone involved. All this to say what almost everyone already knows: implementing change is a painful and costly proposition. But as with anything worth doing, the benefits outweigh the costs. In fact, in the case of a church moving from inactivity to true discipleship, the benefits are so expansive as to render the costs insignificant. Insignificant as they may be in the overall scheme of things, they will nevertheless be painful to endure in the short term.

So what are some of the costs church leaders can expect to pay as they seek to help believers, and in turn the church, become what they were meant to be?

The Price Church Leaders Must Pay

The cost of transfusion and transformation will vary from situation to situation, but there are some things everyone should expect. The first is personal. We leaders often draw our self-worth and sense of significance from the role we play in the body of Christ. We like the respect and admiration of others and find security in the way others depend on us. We like being needed. But if we want to see a movement of multiplying disciples released, we've got to let go of our need to have our egos massaged. We have to deal with our own pride and need for acceptance before we can deal with anything else. We must have faith that Christ has called us to be equippers of equippers. Their success must be valued more than our own.

Leaders will also have to give up some control over order and outcomes. To encourage churchgoers to follow Jesus, leaders will have to stop being the ones with the answers or the ones who plan and execute everything. Instead, leaders have to start insisting that others accept responsibility for their own personal faith and callings. This will make churchgoers insecure and will likely result in verbal assaults or worse for the leadership.

People in traditional churches will simply not understand the changes. They have been conditioned to believe that leadership should be strong and directive, that leaders are responsible for getting things done, and they will be looking for the leader to manage instead of lead. Their focus is on the completion of tasks, not the maintenance and infusion of health. When the leader begins to lead them toward change, there will be a backlash. Leaders must prepare themselves for this eventuality by trusting that God can and will defend them and their reputations. They must be prepared to respond with "gentleness and reverence." There is no reason to take a strident tone and add to the conflict. Instead leaders should calmly reinforce the reason for the new approach to leadership. Take the time to talk with people and assure them that the desired result is a healthy functioning body that can influence the world with the presence of Christ. Remind them that they too are called to minister and that you only want to help them fulfill the destiny for which they were born. It is helpful to preach, teach, talk, and reinforce these truths in any way possible. People will resist at first, but eventually they will begin to understand the wisdom in the new approach.

There will be some who refuse to change and will likely seek a church that allows them to remain docile and irresponsible. They may even garner the support of others in their dissent and lead them out of the church as well. When this happens, the whole church suffers. As we mentioned in Chapter Four, David Gibbons found that his church lost upwards of 40 percent of its people and financial support during its transfusion process. That is a huge price tag for change. Well-meaning members will begin to wonder if the leadership is doing the right thing. They see people they love and respect leaving the church. They then start to question the direction the church has taken. The pressure on leaders to backtrack will be difficult to resist. Here is where a certain resolve to stay the course is absolutely needed. If the leadership flinches at this point, it may not be able to recover. This is why we suggest that pastors spend the necessary time and effort to bring other leaders up to speed and on board before moving fully ahead. A unified leadership team will go a long way toward providing a sense of peace and confidence to the rest of the church.

Peers that you were once close to will also not understand this way of being and doing church. They may even think that you have gone over the edge and lost your sanity. They will not value the same things that you do and will not want to share in the things you are experiencing. The very things you feel must change may come across as an insult to their own ministry values, even when you do not intend anything of the sort. They may even try to make you feel foolish for pursuing this new venture. Family members who are committed to traditional ways of church may no longer support those who are pursuing organic church. In many cases they simply choose not to talk about it anymore when they get together; sadly, in the worst cases they choose not to talk to each other at all.

You will also find that while you knew exactly what to do in the old way of being church, solutions are not as clean in the messier organic church environment. In a church where we lead with programming, the solution to a problem is often direct and clear: get people involved. We could feel good about our success based on people's attendance in the programs. As a result, actual engagement with people was much cleaner and orderly, and we measured our success with clearly defined categories. Not so in a more relational and organic environment. In the old way, if you doubted your effectiveness, you could just get busier and feel better about yourself as you replaced relationships with busyness and project management. In the new way of church, relationships are the core of ministry. Relationships take time and will often lead to disappointment.

Doing church organically is not easier; however, it is simpler and less expensive, and more people can do it. But *easier* would not be our word to describe it. Why? Because organic church can be more painful and require more sacrifice. Organic church is a far more relational way of connecting than the more traditional church experience, and relationships can be painful.

I (Neil) used to read Paul's prayers and emotions for the churches he started and felt inadequate as a pastor because I wasn't as deeply moved by my church as he was by his. I pastored a church that was less organic and therefore less relational. It was still a family, and we loved each other, but we functioned based more on programming than the kind of church I am part of now. When someone fell away, we were sad for a bit. A chair remained empty for a few weeks until someone else came along and filled it. It was common for some to leave and others to come, so it didn't affect our emotions as much over time.

After starting churches from nothing in very dark places, I have come to understand Paul's feelings toward his disciples and church plants. I watched as people caught up in darkness gave their lives over to Christ and became children of God. I walked alongside them as they took their first steps in Christ. I laughed and cried with them as they learned more about Christ and started following him and started following him and received ridicule for it. They were not just parishioners; they were family—but more than that, they were my spiritual children. I finally came to understand what Paul felt for his own spiritual children.

When some of these fell away from Christ, it felt like my own children were abandoning Him. Any parent can relate to that. Sleepless nights of prayer, days full of tears, bellyaches, and a deep longing to do anything to get them to listen and respond to Jesus filled my life at times. This is the higher cost of doing church organically.

A few years ago Neil presented a talk to our movement's conference. He used a reference from the *Matrix* movie that has been a consistent metaphor in our movement. "Taking the red pill" has become common terminology for swallowing organic church ideas and values so that you cannot go back to the way things were before. He titled the talk "Why, Oh, Why, Didn't I Take the Blue Pill? The Darker Side of Organic Church."

In his talk he mentioned many of the costs a leader must bear that have been mentioned here. He started by reading an actual letter he had received from a young church planter in Germany named David who was struggling to see things happen the way he had hoped. In this letter, reprinted below, you will be able to see some of the frustrations that we face when we apply ourselves to organic church. You will notice the sense of frustration, of not knowing when to stop trying to reach a person or group. You will notice the feeling of not knowing if you are doing things right or not. Organic church is messy and not easily measurable. There are hints that David is no longer as connected to the peers as he once was. (It is important to note that shortly after this letter, David saw significant breakthroughs leading the members of a drug-dealing biker gang to Christ and baptizing them, but that's a whole other story.) Here is David's letter:

> Hi, Neil,
> How are you doing?
> I'm not sure about coming in January. I removed myself from the church board a few months ago, so theoretically I could be in Long Beach. I'm just not sure.

In fact I'm not sure about a lot of things these days. It's funny, I have started this e-mail several times now during the last ten days, and I changed it several times as well. Sometimes I wrote "I'm doing OK," sometimes "not well." Today it's probably in between. But these days I cannot say that I'm doing fine.

I think I'm a combination of frustrated, sad, helpless, angry, and tired. We're now about twenty months into the game but still haven't seen a single conversion.

Sure, we're in touch with some people. Just yesterday we had three couples over (in addition to our church people) for a late celebration of my wife's birthday. It was good. We had a nice time with a conversation game I created (questions about life, faith, etc.). Good was also that Satya, after a longer period (in which I felt that he wasn't really seeking anymore and in which we stopped reading the miracles), had asked to meet again to continue our reading.

Good things, but still I feel disoriented and without direction about my role in this whole endeavor. Building relationships is OK, but I don't feel used by God. I'm thinking that Jesus didn't send his disciples out to build relationships but to preach the Gospel. And I have no clue how to do that today.

That leaves me tired. Last week Monday or Tuesday I probably reached my lowest point. I spent time with the Lord; I sang some songs in the midst of tears. I couldn't even put words to my feelings.

I'm tired of leading without having someone who's leading me. The worst part: God has just stayed silent. Didn't say a word about all of this so far.

Sometimes I felt like giving up, but at the same time I knew that I couldn't. First, I knew I couldn't just quit, and second, I wouldn't have anything else to do that would have meaning. I don't feel used as a tool at all. (Which was what God had said during my experience at the beach in Long Beach in April '05). And God doesn't say anything. And sometimes I feel even too tired to again seek the Lord. I don't know what to think.

Sometimes I feel that I'm the wrong guy for the job.
So much from here.
Greetings to you!
David

Leadership is often a lonely proposition, and the path ahead is seldom crystal clear. God often uses the fires of conflict, both internal and external, to forge us into His image. If we trust Him to bring us safely through the problems we face, we will find that He is always faithful to His promises. "He will build His church and the gates of Hell will not prevail against it" (Matt. 16:18b).

THE PRICE CHURCH MEMBERS MUST PAY

Every believer in Jesus is called to take personal responsibility for his or her life—to deny himself, take up his cross daily, and follow Christ. But church members have been conditioned to pass that responsibility off on their leaders. As leaders push that responsibility back during the transfusion process, members become restless. In the famous chapter of the book *The Brothers Karamazov* called "The Grand Inquisitor," the Cardinal, who is interrogating Jesus, accuses Him of making a horrible mistake. It's the Cardinal's belief that Jesus blew it when He died to set men free. The Cardinal believes that it was right, even noble, for the church to take that freedom back because the responsibility of exercising such a freedom was so frightening to humankind. It *can* be a fearful thing to recognize the awesome responsibility that has been given to each and every one of us as believers. It can also be exciting and liberating. We should not imitate the arrogant sin of the church that Dostoevsky describes. The book of Hebrews challenges us to "encourage one another to love and good deeds" (Heb. 10:24). Leaders must look for ways to calm fears and instill a sense of excitement and adventure in each believer so that he or she will willingly accept and pass on the challenge of following Jesus.

When people begin to understand the truth that Jesus is always with them and that He wants to use them to bring good into the world, their perspective on their role in the church begins to change. Be patient with them, and pray for them regularly. The changing of a mind-set is a difficult thing. Without the influence of the Holy Spirit to open eyes and hearts, it is impossible. We believe that God wants this change to occur, so we can count on Him to see it done.

As leaders in the church, we are accustomed to trying to get the people of God to catch the vision for a new direction, but what we usually fail to do is help them calculate the cost. Of course, this is not the case when we are launching a new capital giving campaign, but how often do we actually spell out, in advance, what price people will have to pay for following Christ into a new way of being the church? Jesus spoke clearly about counting the cost before following Him (Luke 14:27–33). We should do likewise in church leadership. Let the people know in advance that you, as leaders, will no longer be doing all the work and that they will need to step forward into ministry. Our friends Dave and Jon Ferguson actually had an ordination service at which the entire church received ordination for the work of ministry. That's not a bad idea. If you do this, be sure to spell out in advance the cost for following Christ. We have found that people respond beyond expectations when they are given the full truth. Encourage your people not just to agree to the vision but also to pay the price, and you will all be better prepared for what is to come.

We might sing the words "I surrender all," but to actually accomplish this is something else altogether. *All* means "all," and that's all that *all* means. The price is pretty steep, but a failure to surrender costs even more. Romans 12:1 encourages all believers to consider God's incredible mercy toward them and, in response to its overwhelming abundance, "present their bodies a living and holy sacrifice to God." I (Phil) once heard Chuck Swindoll say, "The problem with a living sacrifice is that it keeps crawling off the altar." We all crawl off now and then. What's needed is for each of us to surrender ourselves to God in the first place and continue to do so on a regular basis.

THE PRICE DENOMINATIONS MUST PAY

The more your dogma is built on tradition rather than Scripture, the harder your challenge will be. Some evangelical churches do not like to think that they are built on tradition rather than Scripture, but that doesn't mean that they aren't. Just as any family has its own peculiarities, every church does too. It might be something as simple as how people dress or whether or not they can bring drinks into the auditorium, but we all lay a screen of tradition over the way we live out our faith. Written and unwritten denominational rules create fences the Scriptures may never have intended—for instance, rules investing the clergy with special responsibilities reserved only for them, such as the right to baptize or administer communion.

If you have a choice to either follow the Scriptures or the traditions of your denomination, which will you choose? Or which will you be pushed to choose? Believe it or not, there is no denomination that has everything right—each is a bit off in some way. If you think that yours is perfect, you should leave before you spoil it. Every denomination will have some tradition that is slightly at odds with the New Testament. When faced with that, what will you do? Leave? Stay and surrender to what is not biblical? Stay and bring change? Those are your three options.

If you leave, you obviously pay the price of starting over. You might be ostracized and suffer the loss of longtime relationships or at least the pain of strained ones. Once you leave, it might be difficult to find a new church family who will accept you, and those you leave behind will be no closer to following Jesus. Leaving doesn't sound like a great option, but some people may be left with little choice once they've heard the voice of God. Remember, the most important thing is that you listen to Jesus and do what He tells you to do.

If you choose to stay and surrender to what is not biblical, you will pay an even steeper price. This may seem like an odd verse to quote here, so forgive us for being so forward:

> We know that we have passed from death to life, because we love the brothers. He who does not love his brother abides in death. Everyone hating his brother is a murderer. And you know that no murderer has everlasting life abiding in him. By this we have known the love of God, because He laid down His life for us. And we ought to lay down our lives for the brothers. [1 John 3:14–16]

The biblical admonition is clear: love should compel us to lay aside our doubts and fears and seek to help whoever we can to follow Jesus more completely. In Romans 14:16, Paul says, "Don't let what is for you a good thing be spoken of as evil." And six verses later, "Happy is he who does not condemn himself in what he approves." If the Lord has opened your mind to the ideas we are sharing in this book, refusing to act on your newfound insight will have devastating effects on you and those you lead. To go on living under a system you believe is wrong without seeking to do what is right will have a profound effect on your emotional and spiritual well-being. You would find yourself living a double-minded life, and the turmoil that would create for you and for those you lead would be painful indeed.

If you choose to stay and bring change, you will likely be in for a fight. The Scriptures don't lie when they say that a prophet has no honor in his hometown (Mark 6:4). We believe, though, that there are ways to bring change without immediately and directly challenging the status quo. We believe that in most cases it's possible to make and release disciples as Jesus commands without shirking the duties and responsibilities to one's denomination, as we have already pointed out in Chapter Ten.

If you do decide to stay and change, you can expect to be misunderstood and mischaracterized, often by people you love and admire. Just as many in your church might not initially understand, those who are further removed and more institutionally invested will have an even harder time.

Our attempts to share organic concepts within our own denomination have been met with opposition, misunderstanding, and misrepresentation on more than one occasion. Sometimes this has been very painful. Sometimes this was due to our own lack of sensitivity to others and sometimes their lack of sensitivity to us. Either way, the results were the same—hurt feelings and damaged relationships.

Over the past decade, however, there has been a dramatic shift in the conversation. Organic principles are now front and center when we talk about the future of our spiritual family. They're not always called that, and their source is not always acknowledged, but we've witnessed a dramatic shift in the types of issues pastors are willing to address. It's also been good to see that much of the damage done to relationships early on has been repaired and much of the trust has been restored.

Admittedly, our denomination is different from many. We are a fellowship of churches that freely band together based on a common heritage. We have no hierarchical leadership structure to navigate. For us, the main issue is relationships, and we are committed to working hard to preserve these relationships for posterity's sake. If we lose the relationships, we lose the opportunity to have a positive influence on the whole.

The bottom line is that change is hard and pain is probable. Don't be discouraged! "Be steadfast, immovable, always abounding in the work of the Lord, knowing that your toil is not in vain in the Lord" (1 Cor. 15:58).

Any story worth telling is going to be costly. That's just the way it is. Do you want your story to be worth telling? If so, you will have to count the cost and pay the price.

What change could we leave behind if we were all connecting to Jesus and living without traditional boundaries that have kept us boxed up on Sundays behind stained-glass windows? In the Conclusion we will touch on that idea.

Conclusion: Equipping People for Ministry in the World

Why should you want your church to experience transfusion? What should the real goal of a church be? As your church becomes healthier and more missional, what is the potential influence that your church can have? Are we just looking to have more and better churches, or is there another more substantial goal? We believe that the ultimate goal of the church is to love Jesus and demonstrate His holiness, righteousness, grace, and love to the world.

It is our contention that the church in the world has no clue how much potential it really has. It is blind to the impact it is poised to have—if it would only open its eyes and embrace its destiny. It is a sleeping giant preoccupied with simple dreams, all the while missing its true calling and nature.

The church is not what happens on Sunday mornings but what occurs every day of the week in between as believers relate to their Lord, each other, and the people around them. Unfortunately, nearly all our efforts at equipping Christians to serve are focused on what takes place in and through the church's weekly services. Occasionally people are trained to be better spouses or parents, but that may be the extent of the preparation provided for what happens in real life.

We call for volunteers, give them spiritual gift inventories, and in the best churches, work hard to train them to serve, but the target of all that training is most often a better church ministry. People are trained to lead worship, collect and count offerings, greet visitors, care for infants in the nursery, or direct traffic in the parking lot. All of this is good and for the betterment of the church, but it only scratches the surface of what the church should be doing. Some of the best churches will go so far as to train people in evangelism and discipleship, which takes the equipping farther, but we do not believe it takes the people far enough.

If the church is to be all that Paul tells us it is to be in Ephesians 4:1–16, then it must be doing more, much more, to prepare its people to live out the will of God in the world. Our friend and mentor Carol Davis has frequently said, "The church has been preparing the people of God for ministry in the church. It is time to prepare the people of God for ministry in the world."

But is the church able to prepare people to be better doctors, teachers, businesspeople, or civil servants? Yes, but it will not likely be the pastors who will do it. Some of the highest-caliber leaders in every domain of our society are part of the sleeping giant that is the Western church. They likely have little interest in burping babies or passing out bulletins and may not play a musical instrument, so they are not yet being used to the fullest extent. Even if they are being tapped for leadership in the church, it is likely only toward furthering the objectives of the church's internal ministry. But what if the more seasoned lawyers could train the less experienced ones to be better lawyers—and we called it church ministry? Couldn't Christ be served by having much better lawyers in all the fields of law? Not just to be available for churches or even Christians in litigious situations but by simply being better people who advance the legal process for the betterment of society as a whole? Why can't the church ministry be about helping people be better scientists or businesspeople and to practice their vocations with spiritual wholeness?

And that would just be the start of preparing the people of God. When we start blending and mixing the various disciplines and influences of the various domains of society, things will get really interesting. When the Christ-following educators and economists work together to help the Christ-following politicians and civil servants explore ways to strengthen families and teach them how to be self-sufficient and prosperous in the coming economic times, we will start to see some radical ideas begin to shape our culture. The potential for the body of Christ to have significant global impact is incredible when you start to think this way.

What could happen when a Christ-following laboratory scientist who is part of a Presbyterian church in Omaha, Nebraska, under the direction and empowerment of the Holy Spirit, starts communicating with the praying believer who is a doctor in Princeton, New Jersey, and is part of a Pentecostal church? If both are listening and following the Spirit of God in their efforts, is it beyond reason to expect that God can lead His people to find a cure for AIDS? What if these two then start to mix it up with some Spirit-filled businesspeople and a channel of distribution is worked out? It changes the world! We believe that if God's people see their individual vocations as a holy calling in which they are gifted and empowered by the Spirit and are willing to listen to His voice, obey Him, and connect with others who are doing the same, the potential for God's kingdom to influence society is incalculable.

This could really happen if the body of Christ is connected to and taking direction from its Head, listening and following and communicating across all traditional boundaries.

The real question is, does Jesus know how to cure cancer? Does Jesus care about people suffering from cancer? If His people started praying and pleading with Him about these things instead of just focusing on getting more people to attend a worship service on Sunday, what could He do? There is no limit to the unjust and evil conditions in this world that Christ could address through His body if He desires to and His body was listening and obeying.

We believe that the church's best days lie ahead. Our hope is that everyone who names the name of Jesus will choose to courageously follow Him into that future. These believers are yet to awaken to their potential even though they are already deployed and found every day in the very places where they can make the biggest difference. We are in desperate need of a transfusion of Christ's life and a willingness to live together differently so that a new wave of Christ's love and power will be released to affect the world for good. Let's do everything we can to make this happen as soon as possible, and let it begin today—with me.

NOTES

Chapter One: So What's the Difference?

1. Alan Hirsch and Debra Hirsch, *Untamed: Reactivating a Missional Form of Discipleship* (Grand Rapids, Mich.: Baker, 2010), p. 47.
2. Ibid., pp. 45, 47.

Chapter Two: Basic Organic Principles That Work in All Contexts

1. Neil Cole, *Organic Church: Growing Faith Where Life Happens* (San Francisco: Jossey-Bass, 2005), p. 53.
2. Ed Stetzer and Thom Rainer, *Transformational Church,*(Nashville, Tenn.: B&H Publishing, 2010), pp. 36–37.
3. Rick Warren, *The Purpose-Driven Church: Growth Without Compromising Your Message and Mission* (Grand Rapids, Mich.: Zondervan, 1995), p. 102.

Chapter Three: No Longer Business as Usual

1. Jim Collins and Jerry Porras, *Built to Last: Successful Habits of Visionary Companies* (New York: Harper Business, 2004).
2. The only cells without your whole DNA are your reproductive cells, which purposely have only half of your DNA so that they can merge with another's half and form a whole new person.
3. Christian A. Schwarz, *Natural Church Development: A Guide to Eight Essential Elements of Healthy Churches* (Carol Stream, Ill.: ChurchSmart Resources, 1996), p. 10.
4. Roland Allen, *Spontaneous Expansion of the Church and the Causes That Hinder It* (Grand Rapids, Mich.: Eerdmans, 1962), p. 13.
5. Our upcoming book, *Primal Fire,* takes an in-depth look at these five roles and why we need them all to work together for the church to rise in the image of Christ in this world.

6. Ed Stetzer and David Putman, *Breaking the Missional Code: Your Church Can Become a Missionary in Your Community* (Nashville, Tenn.: B&H, 2006), pp. 59–71.
7. Alan Hirsch and Dave Ferguson, in *On the Verge: A Journey into the Apostolic Future of the Church* (Grand Rapids, Mich.: Zondervan, 2011), suggest four steps to transition into an apostolic movement: *imagine, shift, innovate,* and *move.*

Chapter Four: Churches in Transfusion

1. Lawrence O. Richards and Clyde Hoeldtke, *Church Leadership: Following the Example of Jesus Christ* (Grand Rapids, Mich.: Zondervan, 1980).
2. Life Transformation Groups (LTGs) are groups of two or three people of the same sex who meet weekly. The people in the groups choose to read the same book of the Bible that week, approximately twenty to thirty chapters (*divine truth*), confess sins to one another using a list of character conversation questions (*nurturing relationships*), and identify and pray daily for the souls of people not yet following Jesus (*apostolic mission*). You can read more about them in Neil Cole, *Search and Rescue: Becoming a Disciple Who Makes a Difference* (Grand Rapids, Mich.: Baker, 2008). You can also find materials to help you use these groups on our Web site, http://www.CMAResources.org
3. Learn more about XEALOT at http://xealot.org and more about New Song at http://newsong.net

Chapter Five: Dying as if Your Life Depended on It

1. Ray Mayhew, "Embezzlement: The Corporate Sin of Contemporary Christianity," n.d., http://www.relationaltithe.com/pdffiles/EmbezzlementPaper.pdf

Chapter Six: Detoxifying from Dependence

1. Upton Sinclair, *I, Candidate for Governor: And How I Got Licked* (1935) (Berkeley: University of California Press, 1994), p. 109.
2. Dan Heath and Chip Heath, *Switch: How to Change Things When Change Is Hard* (New York: Broadway Books, 2010), p. 4.
3. The passage that is most often cited regarding a pastor feeding the sheep is John 21:15–17, where in the Authorized Version Jesus repeats three times to Peter "Feed my sheep." However, the passage is better

translated as "tend my sheep." Perhaps this translation is another example of some teachers assuming a position of authority over the church that was not meant to be.

4. Neil Cole, *TruthQuest: The Search for Spiritual Understanding* (Signal Hill, Calif.: CMAResources, 2004), http://www.cmaresources.org/node/79

5. Of course, the plan can be adapted for your specific context. We have found that the scenario we describe is the most popular and effective method when working with lay leaders who have both full-time jobs and ministries to manage.

6. We want to mention that neither of us believes that such a licensure process is needed to serve, nor is it in any way a biblical process. We have been doing and learning about organic church for a couple of decades now, and along the way we have put more than a few of our emerging leaders through the licensure process that we have now come to see as superfluous. Those who have been through Truth-Quest have proved quite competent at handling the Scriptures in that context. Please do not think that we are suggesting or endorsing any kind of licensure or ordination process that perpetuates a poor model of clergy or laity in our churches.

7. John M. Glionna, "Japanese Retirees Volunteer to Work in Stricken Nuclear Plant," *Los Angeles Times*, July 4, 2011, http://articles.latimes.com/2011/jul/04/world/la-fg-japan-nuclear-old-20110704

8. "Crystal Cathedral Denies Reports of Schuller's Ouster from Board," *Los Angeles Times*, July 4, 2011, http://latimesblogs.latimes.com/lanow/2011/07/crystal-cathedral-denies-reports-of-schullers-ouster-from-board.html

Chapter Seven: How Small People Cause Big Problems

1. Neil Cole, *Organic Leadership: Leading Naturally Right Where You Are* (Grand Rapids, Mich.: Baker Books, 2009.)

Chapter Eight: Leadershifts

1. Lawrence O. Richards and Clyde Hoeldtke, *Church Leadership: Following the Example of Jesus Christ* (Grand Rapids, Mich.: Zondervan, 1980), p. 195.

2. Rick Warren, *The Purpose-Driven Life: What on Earth Am I Here For?* (Grand Rapids, Mich.: Zondervan, 2002), p. 17.

3. Dee W. Hock, "The Chaordic Organization: Out of Control and into Order," *World Business Academy Perspectives*, 1995, 9(1), http://www

.ki-net.co.uk/graphics/Dee%20Hock%20-%20The%20Chaordic%20 Organization.pdf

4. Richards and Hoeldtke, *Church Leadership*, p. 75.

5. Skye Jethani, "The Evangelical Industrial Complex and the Rise of Celebrity Pastors," *SkyeBox*, February 13, 2012, http://www .skyejethani.com/the-evangelical-industrial-complex-the-rise-of -celebrity-pastors/1166/

6. Bob Hyatt, "The Dangerous Pursuit of Pastoral Fame," *OutofUR.com*, February 13, 2012, http://www.outofur.com/archives/2012/02/the _dangerous_p_3.html#more

Chapter Nine: Disciples, Disciples, Disciples

1. Miguel Labrador, "Discipleship: A Thought," *God Directed Deviations*, http://www.pathwaysinternational.org/2012/01/discipleshipdna

2. Neil Cole, *Cultivating a Life for God: Multiplying Disciples Through Life Transformation Groups* (Signal Hill, Calif.: CMAResources, 1999); Neil Cole, *Search and Rescue: Becoming a Disciple Who Makes a Difference* (Grand Rapids, Mich.: Baker Books, 2008).

Chapter Ten: Water the Green Spot

1. Ralph Winter, quoted in the booklet available at http://www .missionfrontiers.org/uploads/. . ./rdw-booklet-r-butler.pdf

2. Michael Frost and Alan Hirsch, *The Shaping of Things to Come: Innovation and Mission for the 21st-Century Church* (Peabody, Mass.: Hendrickson, 2003), pp. 47–51.

3. William Barclay, *The Gospel of John, Volume 2*, rev. ed. (Philadelphia: Westminster Press, 1975), p. 58.

4. Ray Oldenburg, *The Great Good Place* (New York: Marlowe & Company, 1991).

5. Robert Putnam, *Bowling Alone: The Collapse and Revival of American Community* (New York: Simon & Schuster, 2000).

6. Everett M. Rogers, *Diffusion of Innovations*, 5th ed. (New York: Free Press, 1995), pp. 280–281.

7. Malcom Gladwell, *The Tipping Point: How Little Things Can Make a Big Difference* (New York: Little, Brown, 2000).

8. Alan Hirsch and Dave Ferguson, *On the Verge: A Journey into the Apostolic Future of the Church* (Grand Rapids, Mich.: Zondervan, 2011), p. 100.

Chapter Eleven: Healthy Reproduction

1. Carl George, *Prepare Your Church for the Future* (Grand Rapids, Mich.: Revell, 1991).
2. Geoff Surratt, Greg Ligon, and Warren Bird, *A Multi-Site Church Road Trip: Exploring the New Normal* (Grand Rapids, Mich.: Zondervan, 2009).
3. Ibid., pp. 210–215.
4. George Patterson, "The Spontaneous Multiplication of Churches," in Ralph D. Winter and Steven C. Hawthorne, eds., *Perspectives on the World Christian Movement*, 4th ed. (Pasadena, Calif.: William Carey Library, 2009), p. 642.
5. David Garrison, *Church Planting Movements: How God Is Redeeming a Lost World* (Midlothian, Va.: WigTake Resources, 2004), pp. 21–22.
6. Neil Cole, *Church 3.0: Upgrades for the Future of the Church* (San Francisco: Jossey-Bass, 2010), pp. 85–87.

Chapter Twelve: New Measures of Success

1. Neil Cole, *Church 3.0: Upgrades for the Future of the Church* (San Francisco: Jossey-Bass, 2010), p. 169.
2. Reggie McNeal, *Missional Renaissance: Changing the Scorecard for the Church* (San Francisco: Jossey-Bass, 2009), p. 20.
3. Neil Cole, *Organic Church: Growing Faith Where Life Happens* (San Francisco: Jossey-Bass, 2005), p. xxiii.
4. Ori Brafman and Rod Beckstrom, *The Starfish and the Spider* (New York: Penguin, 2006), pp. 50–51.
5. Quoted in Elmer Towns, Ed Stetzer, and Warren Bird, *11 Innovations in the Local Church: How Today's Leaders Can Learn, Discern, and Move into the Future* (Ventura, Calif.: Regal Books, 2007), p. 25.
6. Alan Hirsch and Debra Hirsch, *Untamed: Reactivating a Missional Form of Discipleship* (Grand Rapids, Mich.: Baker, 2010), p. 45.
7. McNeal, *Missional Renaissance*, p. 65.
8. Leonard Sweet, *Soul Tsunami: Sink or Swim in the New Millennium Culture* (Grand Rapids, Mich.: Zondervan, 1999), p. 16.
9. Mark Galli, "Long Live Organic Church!" *Christianity Today*, January 7, 2010, http://www.christianitytoday.com/ct/2010/januaryweb-only/11-41.0.html

The Authors

Neil Cole is an experienced church planter and pastor as well as an international speaker. In addition to having founded the Awakening Chapels, which are reaching young postmodern people in urban settings, he is also a founder of Church Multiplication Associates (CMA), which has trained more than fifty thousand people in organic church planting over the past eleven years and has churches throughout the United States and in more than forty countries. Neil is also one of the key founding leaders of the simple church movement, which is rapidly growing around the world. Currently Neil serves as executive director of CMAResources. He is responsible for providing church leaders with the ministry tools needed to reproduce healthy disciples, leaders, churches, and movements. His responsibilities also include developing, training, and coaching church planters.

Neil is the author of *Cultivating a Life for God: Multiplying Disciples Through Life Transformation Groups* (1999), *TruthQuest: The Search for Spiritual Understanding* (2004), *Organic Church: Growing Faith Where Life Happens* (2005), *Search and Rescue: Becoming a Disciple Who Makes a Difference* (2008), *Organic Leadership: Leading Naturally Right Where You Are* (2009), *Church 3.0: Upgrades for the Future of the Church* (2010), and *Journeys to Significance* (2011). He is coauthor (with Paul Kaak) of *Organic Church Planters' Greenhouse: The First Story* (2004) and (with Robert E. Logan) of *Raising Leaders for the Harvest* (1995) and *Beyond Church Planting: Pathways for Emerging Churches* (2005). He lives in Long Beach, California, with his wife, Dana, near their three grown children, Heather, Erin, and Zachary.

Phil Helfer is pastor of Los Altos Grace Brethren Church in Long Beach, California. Los Altos is a sixty-year-old church with a traditional skin and an organic soul. Phil is also a founder of Church Multiplication Associates (CMA), where he has served as shepherd for more than twenty years. Phil trains and coaches church planters and speaks to groups locally and internationally. Phil lives in Long Beach, California, with his wife, Lori, and his three daughters, Jenna, Haley, and Stacey.

INDEX

A

Abraham and Isaac, 44

Acts: 1, 16; 1:8, 180; 1:15, 173; 2, 16; 2:41, 173; 5:41, 173; 13:36, 181; 13:49, 173; 16:5, 173; 16:20, 176; 17:6-7, 176–177; 19:20, 173; 19:26, 177; institutional to influential transition in, 173–176

Adam and Eve, 5, 102

Adult Bible Fellowship, 50

Africa, 49

Allen, R., 35, 182

Ambition: faulty decisions caused by, 101–113; selflessness *versus*, 126–127; in story of John and James, 104–113; success and, 183

Andrew, 112

Apollos, 174

Apostle, defined, 20

Apostolic mission: defined, as DNA element, 18, 20; reproduction and, 23; steps for, 200*n.* 2:7

Apprentice-leader approach, 158, 159

Asian American church transfusion, 60–62

Attendance figures, 170, 171, 183

Attractional model: codependence in, 83–86, 93; discipleship *versus,* 56–57; outward orientation *versus,* 34; self-centeredness promoted by, 121

Authority: in Bible, 90–91; of Christ, 121; positional *versus* spiritual/ relational, 96–97, 113, 120–123; positional *versus* submission to, 120–123

Authorized Version, 200*n.* 5:3

Automatic growth parable, 163, 164

Awakening Chapels, 29

B

Barnabas, 43

Beckstrom, 172

Behavior modification, 4–5

Believers. *See* Church members; Disciples

BHAG (Big Hair Audacious Goal), 25

Bible: authority in, 90–91; on clergy, 38; on command to teach, 92–93; on conduct of the church, 31–32, 33, 38; connecting people to, 90–91; on *cosmos,* 116; denominational rules and, 193; mistranslations of, 142, 200*n.* 5:3; on the nature of the church, 14, 15–16, 31; on nurturing relationships, 19; for rules to live by *versus* the truth, 130–133; study versions of, 87. *See also specific book headings*

Big shots, as obstacles to reproduction, 166

Bird, W., 161, 162

Blocking, of incoming hostilities, 146–147

207

World system *(cosmos)*, 116–118,
176–177
Worship service: church's potential
for more than, 196–198;
entertainment factor in, 83–84;
spontaneity in, 154
Wozniak, S., 137
Written enlightenment, 182

X
XEALOT, 62, 200*n*. 3:2

Y
Youth: boundaries for, 143; Godly,
182–183; leadership development
in, 54; in skunk works project,
138–139; spontaneous projects of,
54–56

Z
Zebedee, sons of, 104–113
Zinzendorf, Count, 182

Other Books by Neil Cole

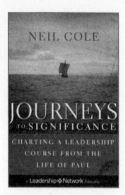

In *Journeys to Significance*, bestselling author and organic church leader Neil Cole takes us on a journey as we follow the life of the apostle Paul and learn valuable lessons about how God forms a leader over the course of his or her life. It's not about just reaching the end—it's about finishing well and keeping your eye on the ultimate goal, not on short-term wins or losses. *Journeys to Significance* provides valuable insights to help any leader (or aspiring leader) to build upon each journey so that finishing strong is not only possible, but is a clear and practical focus in the here and now.

ISBN 978-0-7879-6893-9 | $24.95

In *Church 3.0*, Cole makes the argument that Christianity needs more than new programs, buildings, or worship formats. It needs a complete upgrade to a new operating system. The early church shifted to a more institutional form in 300 AD and has been stuck in the 2.0 operating system ever since. We are overdue for the next upgrade. *Church 3.0* discusses issues such as how to deal with heresy, how to handle finances, what to do with children, and what to do with worship, rituals, and ordinances. Even the most enthusiastic proponents and practitioners of organic churches often wonder how to handle such matters in a faithful way.

ISBN 978-0-7879-9520-1 | $24.95

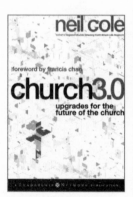

If we want to connect with young people and those who are not coming to church, we must go where people congregate. Cole shows readers how to plant the seeds of the Kingdom of God in the places where life happens and where culture is formed—restaurants, bars, coffeehouses, parks, locker rooms, and neighborhoods. *Organic Church* offers a hands-on guide for demystifying this new model of church and shows the practical aspects of implementing it. While it may seem revolutionary, this model of church—bringing God's message where people are rather than expecting them to show up at church—is in keeping with the message of Jesus, who lived among the people of his time. *Organic Church* shows how we can return to those ancient roots by letting the church be alive, organic, growing, spreading in the most likely and unlikely places.

ISBN 978-0-7879-8129-7 | $24.95